The Myth-Busting Guide to Psychosis

The
Myth-Busting
Guide to
Psychosis

Demystifying Hallucinations,
Delusions, and How to Live Well

Kai Conibear

Foreword by Dr Sameer Jauhar

Jessica Kingsley Publishers
London and Philadelphia

First published in Great Britain in 2024 by Jessica Kingsley Publishers
An imprint of John Murray Press

1

The information contained in this book is not intended to replace the services of
trained medical professionals or to be a substitute for medical advice. You are advised
to consult a doctor on any matters relating to your health, and in particular on
any matters that may require diagnosis or medical attention.

Content Warning: this book mentions bipolar disorder, loss of a loved one,
schizophrenia, substance abuse, and suicide.

A CIP catalogue record for this title is available from the British Library
and the Library of Congress

ISBN 978 1 83997 866 1
eISBN 978 1 83997 867 8

Printed and bound in Great Britain by CPI Group

Jessica Kingsley Publishers
Carmelite House
50 Victoria Embankment
London EC4Y 0DZ

www.jkp.com

John Murray Press
Part of Hodder & Stoughton Ltd
An Hachette Company

Contents

Foreword

It was a pleasure both to be asked to write this foreword and – more importantly – to read this book. I had never met Kai before, but we were put in contact with each other through Bipolar UK, a charity we both make time for.

To my mind, writing about mental illness is not easy. In *The Myth-Busting Guide to Psychosis*, Kai succeeds in creating a book that I finished at the first sitting – something that rarely happens to me these days.

I have worked clinically with people with severe mental illness and their families for over 20 years, and for the last decade with people with first episode psychosis, a significant number of whom have bipolar disorder. The problems that people encountered when I started as a trainee – misunderstanding, stigma, misinformation, amidst the challenges of these illnesses themselves – have not gone away. In fact, in the modern era of social media, they have probably been magnified. It is in this context that I welcome this book.

In the first section Kai tackles head-on the term psychosis, and gives a very clear definition, as well as introducing concepts associated with the term, its effects on the individual and those close to them. He also takes the opportunity to introduce the views of those he has interviewed, who have psychosis.

Myths, such as people with psychosis being dangerous and needing to be looked after in hospital for the majority of their lives, are dealt with in a clear and concise fashion.

Kai then goes on to cover what psychosis actually is and gives as clear a description of psychotic symptoms as one would get from one of our psychiatry textbooks.

Stigma is the next topic, and is again covered with brutal honesty. Specifically, he covers this within the workplace, social media, friendships, and families.

By offering solutions to these various problems, gleaned from his own and others' perspectives, a welcome degree of optimism is maintained, and practical solutions are emphasized (some of which I have stolen).

In conclusion I have to say this is a strong piece of work which benefits from not only Kai's individual experience, but from the interviews with others and reflections on the wider issues, as well as probably the right amount of evidence from the literature.

I wish this book had been around for people when I was a trainee and would have little hesitation in recommending it for my trainees, colleagues, and more importantly those with psychosis and their families.

Dr Sameer Jauhar
Senior Clinical Lecturer in Affective Disorders and Psychosis, King's College London

PART I
MYTH-BUSTING PSYCHOSIS

Psychosis is not a mental illness but a symptom that appears as part of different mental illnesses. It can also be caused by some physical illnesses, injuries, and substance misuse. There are many misconceptions about what it means to live with psychosis. With two decades of experience with psychotic symptoms, I've heard it all. At least, I feel as though I have! What continues to surprise me is where I hear these stigmatizing ideas coming from. Often, it's from people I've known for years. People with past experiences of mental illness or who continue to live with one. Individuals with a vast wealth of life experience and highly educated individuals. Even from close family and friends to whom I've explained in detail what psychosis is and what it definitely isn't, and who have witnessed me in the middle of a psychotic episode. The scope of the lack of knowledge and education surrounding psychosis is staggering. And it's everywhere – and I mean everywhere. From tabloids to broadsheets, TV and film, books, and music, psychosis is misrepresented throughout popular culture and in the news we consume daily.

The reality is skewed and distorted to fit different narratives and opinions that ignore the real people who have and will continue to experience psychosis.

So I could sit in my little corner of the internet and write grumpy blog entries or Twitter/X threads into the void. Or I could step up and support others like me and put something positive out into the world – this book.

The general lack of knowledge about psychosis has a massive impact on those who have psychosis. It creates stigma and discrimination which distorts how the people in their lives see psychosis, and creates division and fear. People with psychosis often feel isolated, alone, and severely depressed, which unfortunately can exacerbate symptoms. This book is about busting these myths that create division and empowering people with psychosis to navigate those sometimes difficult conversations about stigma. In Part I, we'll be exploring what psychosis is, looking at delusions and hallucinations, and busting some common myths about this often-misunderstood condition.

Note: Throughout this book, I include interviews from a diverse group of people, who all have lived experience of psychosis. Certain words used to describe being mentally unwell or psychotic are part of these interviews. Some people are comfortable using them while others are not. Where these words are included, they've been retained to keep the interviewee's voice authentic.

Chapter 1

What Is Psychosis?

What everyone wants to ask, but they're not sure how

With psychosis, there's this feeling you get.

It's that feeling when eyes are on you; you can physically feel them, almost as if the heat and pressure from that gaze could cause real pain. It's gnawing at you, uncomfortable and claustrophobic. It's so oppressive that you feel the need to get up and leave the room, go to the bathroom, or get some fresh air outside so you can breathe freely again.

This is what psychosis can feel like.

But that's also what it can feel like when you tell someone you have psychosis, or they find out. Their eyes widen. They look confused, awkward, even scared.

Whatever your experiences, this book is here to demystify psychosis. It's for anyone with psychosis who has tried and failed to be understood, or who has struggled to debunk the many misconceptions surrounding the hallucinations and delusions that make up a psychotic episode. But it's also for the curious and the people who genuinely want to understand, learn, and be an accepting and compassionate ally for people with psychosis.

I could spend pages and pages explaining what psychosis is from a medical point of view, but that won't solve the problems that people living with psychosis face. There's understanding something and then there's understanding on a deep, emotive level that allows people to see others beyond a symptom or a label. And for people with that symptom to live better, happier lives.

In the past decade, there has been an active push to destigmatize mental illnesses. Charities, campaigners, and activists have worked hard to raise awareness, and people seem more open to talking about common mental health conditions such as depression and anxiety. However, while perceptions have shifted, many people still hold stigmatizing beliefs: 'Over a third of the public think people with a mental health issue are likely to be violent' (Time to Change 2015).

This trend hasn't gone away, with research showing that stigma against psychosis profoundly affects people's lives and wellbeing and their ability to seek treatment and support.

The findings suggest that independent of symptom severity, perceived stigma may contribute to delay in seeking treatment for FEP (First Episode Psychosis), and this delay may amplify the deleterious effects of stigma on psychological functioning. The results point to the importance of reducing DUP (Duration of Untreated Psychosis) and validating interventions targeting the psychological effects of stigma in people with FEP. (Mueser *et al.* 2020)

When explaining to someone you have psychosis, it's difficult when someone says something like, 'Oh, I've only heard that word used in that show where the murderer is "psychotic". Can you explain it to me?' Let's be honest; it's not the easiest starting point. It's an intimidating 'I want to pull my hair out' place to start a dialogue about psychosis. It can honestly feel exhausting to keep saying the same things repeatedly. This is where I hope this book will help.

I wasn't aware I had psychotic symptoms until I was in my early 20s when I slowly began to realize that those weird encounters with disembodied voices only I could hear and those weeks full of an irrationally bloated ego boost that I'd had since I was 17 were probably, definitely, signs of psychosis. A cocktail of a lack of basic knowledge, limited interaction with mental health professionals, and a massive glug of denial had stopped me from seeing the truth. When I was diagnosed with bipolar disorder type 1 at 26, I felt I could finally fit the pieces together, and I spoke to a real person about my psychotic symptoms for the first time. Since then, no one has been able to shut me up. First, as a blogger, then a journalist, a mission of mine has been to speak candidly about psychosis. I wanted to open the discussion up to people who may have never encountered this word before or interacted with someone with this symptom of mental illness. It's been unforgiving, deeply frustrating, and unsettling at times, but I've continued to stay determined that raising awareness of psychosis will improve the lives of people like me.

It would be easy to just write about my own experiences, but that's not representative of everyone with psychosis. I can't speak for others and explore all the messy, raw emotions of their stories. I can't adequately explain all the subtleties in their experiences or express the frustration and vulnerability that stigma and discrimination cause. So, throughout this book, I'll share interviews with people from all walks of life who have had experiences of psychosis. They're various voices from different backgrounds and ethnicities, some are part of the LGBTQ+ community, and some live with disabilities and chronic illnesses. My conversations with this diverse group of people have meant a greater range of advice and tips than I could have ever provided on my own. Throughout the book, you'll hear from Michelle, Hazel, Chris, Sam, Kody, Sara, Jen, and Libby, who bring their unique perspectives and experiences that have shaped their personal views on stigma. Our chats won't only focus on their stories and experiences but on advice that's been real-world tested, from how they manage stigma to tried and tested techniques they use in their everyday lives.

THAT word

Let's address the elephant in the room. That word – 'psychosis' – and its friends – 'delusional' and 'psycho'. It's a daunting word if this is the first time you've come across it. It's also a daunting word if you've heard it a thousand times, especially if you're the one having to explain what it means yet again. So, in this chapter, we'll look at the word and its meaning.

Psychosis is not a defined mental illness. Instead, it's a symptom such as insomnia, anxiety, a lack of concentration, depression, or disassociation. You're more likely to experience it as a symptom if you have a mental illness like schizophrenia, schizoaffective disorder, or bipolar disorder, although some people feel psychosis significantly impacts their lives to the point that it feels like a condition in its own right. Because it's a symptom and not a diagnosed mental illness, people don't hear about it as often when we talk about mental health.

Psychosis is defined as losing contact with reality or perceiving the world differently from the people around you. It manifests as hearing, seeing, or feeling things which aren't there, called hallucinations. Or delusions, where people believe something that couldn't possibly be true and has no basis in reality. I'll go into more detail about hallucinations and delusions in Chapters 3 and 4.

The BIG problem with that word is how it is often confused. Its meaning is switched up in different environments and situations. You might hear it incorrectly used to describe someone dangerous. Or to describe someone who has a view, ideology, or political leaning someone disagrees with.

Jen, who had a psychotic episode shortly before her bipolar type 1 diagnosis, had never experienced anything like it. Jen struggled with a paranoid delusion that led to her arrest and six months spent in a prison mental health unit.

> I suppose the weirdest question I've been asked is: am I dangerous? People associate psychosis with violence. And because I committed a crime when I was unwell, that's the question they always ask: were you dangerous when it happened?

I asked Jen how she answered these difficult questions.

> I was a danger to myself and others for a short period because of my psychosis. But it got resolved through medication, and I was more of a danger to myself than to others. I think that's something that people don't get. They hear the word and think, that person is dangerous. It was really difficult to know what to say because it's really difficult to talk about the criminal aspect of the illness because I'd never done anything criminal before. It was the first time. People are always interested in that aspect, the extreme stuff.

I've heard 'psychotic' used to explain an ex's behaviour after a bad breakup or 'delusional' to discredit someone's opinion or intelligence. It's become a minefield of crossed wires and untangling ingrained views to reach a point where you can explain the word 'psychosis'. Often it feels like the meaning is hidden from the mainstream and the general public, which makes it feel as if you're starting a metre behind everyone else in a hundred-metre sprint.

Sara has a diagnosis of schizophrenia and has noticed the often probing and invasive questions people ask her about psychosis.

> I think the weirdest thing for me is people asking if having psychosis makes me a violent or harmful person to be around. It doesn't confuse me that people make that assumption because I know that it's a widespread one. But it just feels like a very odd thing to ask a person who's maybe said that they're experiencing these things. Obviously, there are so many stereotypes about being violent and what people are like during psychosis. But it still always feels incredibly intrusive to me for someone to say that to you.
>
> There's an automatic assumption about psychosis that it must be violent, or it must make you a danger to be around people. And they wouldn't ask that about any other mental health condition. Why they would jump to that conclusion straightaway, it's like, 'OK, right, thanks!'

I'll be looking more closely at the link between psychosis and violence in the next chapter, as we bust the most common myths about psychosis.

Explaining the word 'psychosis' means one thing: questions. Lots and lots of questions. Anticipating those queries and planning ahead will make you feel more in control of the conversation and less directed by random questions and statements.

Feeling off guard makes us hesitate and confuse our words and generally makes us feel we can't properly explain ourselves.

Chris, who lives with schizophrenia, and manages his psychosis through his own art therapy, knows all too well that you can't prepare for every question thrown at you.

> One of the strangest questions I've been asked is, do the voices, or the faces, stay with you during sexual intercourse? When I saw it a few times in my Question and Answer on TikTok, the only way I can answer that is truthfully. Voices don't turn off for those things. So I'm uncomfortable with that. But I can understand how that's quite a loaded question.

I asked Chris, who has 1.5 million followers on TikTok, how he coped with so many intrusive questions.

> I don't feel like it's intrusive for me because I just want to answer questions as best as possible. And I think that they asked that question just to be facetious, or they're doing it just because they want attention because there's a lot of those questions too.

Sometimes the questions we're asked have no easy answer, or a particular view, or opinion is wrapped up in someone's belief system. Kody, a mental health advocate and speaker, uses social media to share his story of living with schizophrenia.

> I specifically get a lot of people who will ask me about whether I believe my psychosis is demons or spiritual awakenings. I find that the strangest because I don't know, even if someone believes that, I don't know why they would feel the need to ask someone struggling with psychosis if that's what they believe it is. Because I think that can be really dangerous to people who

experience delusions and paranoia. So, I think that's probably the weirdest one I constantly get, people asking if I believe that my psychosis or hallucinations are because of demons or some spiritual-related phenomenon.

It's a really difficult one, because some people feel very strongly about it, so I asked Kody if he had any advice for anyone if they do get that question.

I tend to be someone who doesn't feed into those questions a lot. Because I do social media, I found that if I do address those, I get them more and more. I've actually just tried moving past the comments into something that is more tangible. So, I'll still be willing to answer questions or talk about my schizophrenia or psychosis, but I'll avoid anything that I feel would be a danger to me or that I feel may lead into delusions for me.

Below, I've put together how to have a conversation featuring some of the most frequently asked questions people new to psychosis ask – and where that conversation is likely to lead. Are you worried about telling someone you have psychosis and want to be prepared? Or do you want to learn more but are worried about starting that conversation from the very basics? See it as a template for both sides of the conversation. Add your experiences to the answers to show how they relate to you.

'I don't really understand what psychosis is. Can you explain it to me?'

'Psychosis is a term used to explain hallucinations and delusions.'

'OK, but what are hallucinations?'

'Hallucinations can include hearing (auditory), seeing (visual), feeling (tactile) things that aren't really there. There are more types than this, and they're different for everyone.'

I know that feeling. It's like when you're home alone, and you hear a mystery sound, or when you're half asleep in bed, and you see or hear something that makes you jump wide awake.'

'Everyone has those sorts of experiences, but hallucinations are different. They can happen when you're awake, alone or with a group. You can't control when they'll happen or what you hear, see, or feel. When it happens, it's difficult to tell what is real and what is a hallucination.'

'What are delusions?'

'Believing something that isn't true, feeling paranoid, or feeling like you are better than everyone.'

'That doesn't sound so bad. I've definitely felt that way before! Everyone feels like that sometimes.'

'It's more like, "I figured out the formula to time travel." Or "I believe all the photographs in my room have secret cameras." It can feel frightening and disorientating, and you are convinced that what you believe is real.'

'Can you have hallucinations and delusions?'

'Yes. Some people experience both, but others may only have one type of hallucination or delusional thinking.'

Who can experience psychosis? A handy guide

Spoiler: A ton of people during their lifetime.

Psychosis is more common than people realize. According to the National Institute of Mental Health (2023), 100,000 new cases of psychosis are reported each year in the United States. In the UK, 6 per cent of the population say they have experienced at least one symptom of psychosis (McManus *et al.* 2016).

Research suggests that 9.8 per cent of children and young people have experienced symptoms of psychosis. (Healy *et al.* 2019). Psychosis usually first emerges in young people between the ages of 15 and 30 (Drake *et al.* 2016).

Let's break it down further. As I've already said, psychosis can be a symptom of mental illness. You may experience psychosis if you have any of these mental illnesses:

- schizophrenia
- schizoaffective disorder
- bipolar disorder
- post-traumatic stress disorder (PTSD)
- postnatal depression and/or psychosis
- severe depression
- dissociative identity disorder.

But you can experience psychosis without ever being diagnosed with a mental illness. Causes can include:

- sleep deprivation
- trauma
- severe stress
- certain prescription medications
- misuse of alcohol and other drugs

- a few general medical conditions – such as a head injury or an illness, disorder or infection affecting the brain.

How to start a conversation about psychosis – from both sides

You know that moment when you see someone desperate to ask you something. Or they look as if they might burst if they hold in what they need to say any longer. The problem is they can't entirely untangle their thoughts enough to get out what they want to say. You know they're desperate to ask you. You can tell from their body language and probing questions that are just vague enough to keep them from feeling embarrassed. How do you get past the awkward silences and everything that goes unspoken? Or that feeling when the words are replaying in your head, but you can't force yourself to say them? A solid barrier is stopping you from speaking and making yourself heard.

Michelle, who has her own mental health clothing line and a pop-up store in New York to spread awareness of mental health conditions, has had hundreds of conversations about psychosis.

People are always gonna ask. A lot of people are like, 'I have a question. I don't know if it's appropriate.' I'm like, 'Somebody's already asked me – just ask!'

Michelle has a diagnosis of schizophrenia and has found telling the truth is the easiest way to start a conversation.

I find if you just answer the truth, it works. You don't have to beat around the bush, just start saying, 'Well, if I miss this med, or this or that…' You just say 'no (I'm not dangerous)'. If people ask weird questions, just say it like it is.

Sam lives in the UK and has a degree in English Literature. Sam knows how important it is to have these conversations and has her own way of breaking through the barrier.

> I tend to have a spiel which I repeat over and over for people. I want to educate people, but it does get tiring to repeat this over and over. When it comes to writing about my experiences, though, it's almost like a way of therapeutically helping me process them and helping others feel less alone and better understand at the same time. I think I'm just more suited to writing than speaking as a person.

How to start a conversation with someone who wants to learn more about psychosis

We all tend to build up stuff we're worried about – we play out the worst-case scenarios in our heads, anticipate the negative reaction we'll receive and, of course, feel as if the world will end if any of the above comes true. The problem is this: when we tell ourselves it's a big deal, that's how everyone else will see it. When we're planning to share with someone that we experience psychosis, and we fret and agonize and build it up into an event, or a crescendo of anxiety, then we've already told that person this is BIG, this is SCARY, without having said a word.

HOW DO YOU START?

- Choose a casual setting. Your first thought might be lunch together…coffee shop…a sit down somewhere comfy with some privacy. On the surface, these sound perfect. When you're sitting face to face, the eye contact and the intimacy of just the two of you sitting together can be overwhelming. It's too much, too intense, and can paralyze you into silence. The workaround? Go for a walk together. Walk to the shops to pick up some bits or walk round the park together on your lunch break. Or, if that's not your style, bring it up when you're doing an activity together. With both versions, the pressure is off. You're not stuck staring at each other. It doesn't feel like the only reason you've met up is to talk. It creates a casual atmosphere where you can say what you need to say. It gives you the space to focus on something else, which gives you time to think, calm yourself down, and bring into focus how you want to approach this conversation.

- It's a conversation, not a speech. You don't need to list every experience or explain in minute detail what a hallucination or delusion feels like to you. Think of it like this: how would you like it explained to you? Maybe you've been on the other side of a similar conversation. Less is definitely more.

- Don't try to explain everything at once. As I've already said, there may be questions. And then follow-ups. Then more questions. Give them space to hear what you've said and answer their questions. They might not have questions straight away and are the type of person who needs time to process before they send you a barrage of queries. You might feel that desperate need to be understood right now. But this conversation will hopefully be the first of many – the type of chats where it pops up casually, and you feel safe and secure enough with your loved one to tell them how it is, without fear or through a filter.

How to let someone know you're OK to hear more about psychosis

You also have a part to play if you're on the other side of the conversation. All of the above about how the first conversation is built up has much to do with stigma.

Libby, a psychology student from the UK, who has had several psychotic episodes and lives with complex PTSD, finds people hesitate to ask them questions about psychosis, so these important conversations never get started.

> I don't think anyone's really ever asked me questions about it. A part of me feels maybe people are too scared to ask questions sometimes. People don't know what to ask. I guess people assume they know what it is. But they don't. So they don't really know what to ask.

It doesn't necessarily mean they feel you will definitely react badly, but past experiences tell them it's possible. Your part is to show them they can open up to you and make them feel safe and secure enough to start talking.

Hazel, who hears voices and has delusions, explains 'the look' they get when talking about psychosis.

> Most people just change the subject, in my experience. They just seemingly panic. You can see their eyes change. And you can see they're thinking, 'Wow, can I talk to you about something else now?!' The usual response from them is, 'What are you doing this weekend?'

So how do you put their mind at ease? How do you make it clear they can talk to you openly about psychosis, and you won't freak out?

- Give them room to speak.
- Make sure they know you've heard what they've told you.

That can be repeating back (in your own words) what they've explained about psychosis.

- Ask questions. It's OK to ask for more information or for them to clarify what's been said.
- Do your own research about psychosis – then ask them to clarify what you've read and if it relates to their experience.
- Don't make assumptions or act like you know it all – because you don't.
- Be honest. If you don't understand something, speak up and tell them!

How to tell someone you're not ready for that conversation

We all have that perceptive friend who knows something is up. They know what's wrong, and they're waiting for you to come to them. Sometimes they might even confront you if they feel that will help. If you're not ready to talk about psychosis, that's your prerogative. There should never be pressure to talk about it to anyone if you're not ready. It's your choice when and if you share, not theirs. It's important to get this message across to them. It's not that you're being rude or evasive; it's about looking after yourself. I've dealt with this in the past simply by saying, 'I'm not ready to talk about this. Please respect how I feel.'

And that should be all you need to say. It will probably be awkward. You'll feel uncomfortable, but if they care for you, they will respect your decision.

Boundaries

'Boundaries' is just a fancy term for explaining the limits you set with people in a way that keeps you safe and healthy. Those limits you set and stick to should improve your relationships, too. When setting boundaries about how we talk about and what we choose to share about psychosis, things can get complicated. Psychosis is tough to talk about, and many of us who experience it feel overwhelmed by just the idea of opening up. Often, our conversations have started at the very basics. Why? Because many people don't have a frame of reference for psychosis. For all of us, when we try to empathize with someone, we try to put ourselves in their shoes. But what if the shoe doesn't fit? Or worse, what if you've never been taught to tie shoelaces? How can you begin to understand if you can't even wear the shoe?

Chris summed it up during our chat.

> Psychosis is one of those things that freaks people out who haven't been through it themselves. I've noticed that. People can act insane around you, ironically, and you watch other people lose their minds at just the thought that someone hears voices. That's more my thing. Every time I talk to people, I feel like I scare them.

When we find someone who is receptive and has put their judgements and preconceived notions aside to listen to us, we tend to overshare. We're not even thinking about implementing boundaries. It's easy to get carried away and overshare. It's something that Hazel struggles with.

> I am potentially too open. I blame the ADHD! I am a notorious oversharer. So, if anything, sometimes maybe I share things that I shouldn't. There are certain things I won't talk about, but they're not things that people would bring up very often. I tell people I hear voices, and I tell people that I have some degree of delusions, but people very rarely ask for follow-up information.

Or if they do, it's surface level. There are certain beliefs I've had in the past that are just so out of character for me and so horrible that I just don't want to tell anyone because I think people might judge me. Other than that, I'm pretty open, maybe too open at times.

It's important to remember that boundaries are there to keep us safe and well. Individuals with psychosis don't owe others an explanation, and it should not be their responsibility to educate others.

Even when we're in the middle of a conversation, it's still OK to stop, take a step back, and think about whether we're equipped to talk about psychosis at that moment. Carrying on when I know I should stop talking is something I've been guilty of many times. Often, I'm so concerned that my friends and family understand what I'm going through that I end up reliving a stressful psychotic episode just to prove a point. It's never worth it, and I'm left feeling stressed out, uncomfortable, and vulnerable. With social media, it's become easier than ever to tell your story and share it through a medium you find comfortable. Through photos, videos, and the written word, we're now able to share our point of view. It can become damaging when we start to feel we owe our followers more about our lives and ourselves. It can cross over to no longer being cathartic but damaging to our mental wellbeing. Here's where boundaries become so important, as Kody explains.

I've had people ask me to describe hallucinations, which, depending on how I'm doing, I'm not unwilling to do. But if I'm not doing very well, or if I recently had hallucinations, or an episode, I'll usually avoid getting into specifics of what my hallucinations look or sound like. Just because I don't want it to be triggering if I've recently come out of an episode. It can be stressful. I can't even say I can remember having an experience where talking about it led to symptoms. But I think if it's fresh out of me experiencing some form of hallucinations, or me experiencing some sort of paranoia, I get too stressed to talk about it. So I find if I had just recently dealt with symptoms, it's easier for me to avoid those conversations.

Even with family or friends we've built trust with, we still need to set limits. Libby explains how important it is to stick to boundaries once you've set them.

I try to explain things from my perspective. I always make sure that they understand it's different for everyone. And while we may have a general consensus of what it's like, everyone experiences psychotic symptoms differently. It can be harder, depending on the person. It's knowing your boundaries. You don't have to educate everyone. It can be nice if you can, but you don't have to. Make sure you set boundaries and stick to them. I feel if you make exceptions for a boundary, you then start to do it all the time. And then it's no longer a boundary; it's disappeared. So stick to your boundaries, and make sure that you've got some self-care for yourself as well. When you have these questions, even if you don't want to tackle them, you still need to look after yourself. That's really important.

We all want the people we love to understand us. Psychosis complicates things, and we don't always feel understood. This creates barriers to communication, and it can feel very isolating. A good starting point is having clear boundaries in how we communicate, which Sara does with her family and friends.

I've got to a point where I'm able to be open about that with my family, friends and some of my work colleagues. So I think the best thing for me is open communication about what upsets you, and any kind of particular things that might cause stress or might trigger you. I think being honest about what those are to those people might help them, and then they avoid doing those things to upset you. If someone's asking me about stuff, and I don't feel comfortable, I'll just tell them that I feel uncomfortable and then maybe recommend that they look at some sort of online resources, if they've got them available. It is hard, but I think communication is key.

Here are a few points to think about when setting boundaries around conversations about psychosis:

- Think about what you find stressful when talking to people about psychosis.
- Think about how you would like to be spoken to about psychosis and what you find unacceptable.
- Be clear.
- If you're open with someone once, you don't have to be again.
- If someone makes you feel uncomfortable, you don't need to explain why.
- Telling someone 'I don't want to talk about this' should be all you need to say.
- Stick to the boundaries you've set.
- You can implement different boundaries for different people in your life.
- You can change and add to your boundaries if you feel uncomfortable.

Chapter 2

Myth-Busting Psychosis

Probably the biggest hurdle facing those of us trying to explain psychosis is when we encounter myths and misconceptions. It's a massive stumbling block when you find yourself challenging somebody's preconceptions – often, there are multiple preconceptions to deal with before you can even begin to explain what psychosis actually is. It's time-consuming, frustrating, and so much hard work.

I asked each of my interviewees the same question:

'What are the top three misconceptions people hold about psychosis?'

There are more than three myths about psychosis, which became obvious during our interviews. Our chats were casual, and as we talked, more and more of these misconceptions came to light. There was a clear winner, but what was interesting was our interviewees had come across very similar myths, despite living in different countries and coming from varying socioeconomic and cultural backgrounds:

- Psychosis is unrelatable.
- It only happens when you're young.
- People with psychosis are faking or trying to get out of something.
- People with psychosis are stupid/dumb/not capable.
- Every voice you hear is nasty or negative.
- People with psychosis don't want to take part in society.
- Psychosis is the same as having multiple personalities.

I'm old enough to remember when *Top of the Pops* was relevant, so I'm writing this top three with the TOTP countdown playing in my head. Here are our top three.

At number three!

'People with psychosis are always ill and should be in the hospital.'

Coming in at number two:

'People with psychosis can't function in society.'

And top of the charts this week (and every week for a very, very, very long time – longer even than Bryan Adams' hit single from the early 1990s '(Everything I Do) I Do It for You') is:

'People with psychosis are dangerous and violent.'

In this chapter, we'll take a detailed look at each of these misconceptions, why they might exist, and how we can challenge these outdated myths.

Let's start with those myths that just missed out on the top three.

Psychosis is the same as having multiple personalities

This is a common misconception. Dissociative identity disorder (DID), which used to be called multiple identity disorder, has its own symptoms that are distinct from psychosis. The idea that psychosis causes a 'split' personality or multiple personalities is untrue. How you perceive the world around you, whether it's because of a hallucination, a delusion, or both, is altered. It's a confusing and sometimes scary experience, so how you react to situations and other people will, unsurprisingly, be different from how you would normally react.

Psychosis is unrelatable

Have you ever experienced a very vivid dream, maybe one that involves people you know or a situation that could realistically happen? You wake up from that dream, and your first thought is 'Did that really happen, or was it a dream?' It takes a while to filter through what you dreamt and what is real. You might even have to ask someone for clarification so you can be sure.

We all go through strange experiences throughout our lives that we never find an explanation for. Although dreaming or hearing and seeing something unexplained is not the same as an episode of psychosis, it can give someone a glimpse of what it might be like.

One of the reasons people believe psychosis isn't relatable is the belief that it's extremely rare. Psychosis and psychosis-related disorders are more common than many people think. According to the National Alliance on Mental Illness (NAMI 2023), in the US, there are approximately 100,000 new cases of psychosis each year, and three in 100 people will have an episode of psychosis at some point in their lives. In the UK, the numbers are lower at one in 100 (Rethink Mental Illness 2023), but surveys focusing on psychosis are few and far between, and this number doesn't take into consideration people in hospitals, prisons, or sheltered housing, or the homeless. The actual number is probably higher. Kody shared with me why he believes people have such a hard time accepting that psychosis is more common than they believed.

> I think it's because a lot of people are able to function better than how the media portrays people with psychosis. So when they hear 'psychosis', they have a very distinct image of what it is based on what they've seen in either the news media, TV shows, or movies, and as people living with schizophrenia or psychosis know, it's not at all like that, especially if you're someone who is well medicated and been through treatment. So I think there are a lot of people living very full lives. And a lot of those people, because of the stigma surrounding it, aren't sharing that with everyone in their life. So, the chances are people are meeting other individuals with schizophrenia or psychosis, and probably never finding out because those people are too nervous about the stigma surrounding it or embarrassed to talk about it. That's why I believe that people think it's more rare than it actually is – it's because I don't think people understand how commonly they may be interacting with people who are struggling with psychosis or schizophrenia.

It only happens when you're young

As I mentioned in Chapter 1, the onset of the first episode of psychosis is usually between the ages of 15 and 30. People presume psychosis happens when you're a teenager. For Jen, this wasn't the case.

It happened to me when I was slightly older. I was 27. And people think it just happens in your teenage years or early 20s. But for me, it happened when I was 27. So it can happen later on in life. It just happened out of the blue. And that was my first episode. So yeah, they (friends and family) were quite confused, to be honest.

People with psychosis are faking or trying to get out of something

Psychosis has been played out over and over again on TV and in film, and if you pay attention, the message that's repeated is it's pretty easy to convince anyone that you're psychotic. Even high-profile serial killers back in the 1980s tried to convince the authorities they were psychotic so they would be sent to a hospital instead of prison. Hazel has noticed that this myth negatively affects people's views of psychosis.

People believe that we're malingerers or trying to get out of something because people seem to think that if someone's arrested, and they plead insanity, they're actually faking it. And people seem to think that psychosis is easy to fake. According to every psychiatrist I've ever spoken to and every research paper I've ever read, psychosis is not easy to fake, but the general public seems to think you sit in a corner and talk to yourself, and then you get to go to a hospital rather than prison. We had a thing recently (near me) where someone damaged a shop. In the newspaper, it was talking about how he had psychosis and no one had done anything. And it was a failure of the health service. Almost all the comments were saying, 'I bet he wasn't actually ill; I bet he was just drunk.' 'People just use mental illness as an excuse so much these days' – and that's what almost all the comments were.

It would be extremely difficult to fake an episode of psychosis and to keep that façade up for more than a couple of hours.

People with psychosis are stupid/dumb/not capable

There's this preconceived notion that if you have any kind of psychosis, you're not smart or capable. You're slow to think, shuffling along as you walk, and not able to even hold a conversation. It often comes from the idea that people with psychosis are always heavily drugged and sedated. Psychosis alters how you see the world, and sometimes it affects how you react to others. During an episode of psychosis, it might manifest as disordered speech or problems communicating when you're very unwell. Chris explains how people with this idea interact with him.

> Another barrier I've encountered is people think I'm stupid. Sometimes they talk to me, and then they're, really slowly, 'Hello.' I'm like, 'Hi. What?' They think because you have something that you're just gonna be this pitiful person walking around and doing whatever, but it's not so.

Although during an episode of psychosis, we might not be capable of looking after ourselves, attending school or university, or working, that doesn't mean we aren't smart, capable individuals. People with psychosis achieve academically and are talented and creative individuals with vibrant ideas – even the person writing this book has experienced psychosis!

Every voice you hear is nasty or negative

Libby explains how voice hearing can be a positive experience for some people with psychosis.

[People believe] every voice you hear is nasty. And horrible. Or it's always telling you to hurt other people. That's a huge misconception. Sometimes, they're not mean; they're not nasty. They're just annoying. Sometimes, they make no sense. Sometimes they can be nice. I think a lot of people don't talk about how sometimes hallucinations can actually be quite nice to you. I've never really had ones that are nice to me. But I know quite a few people who have, and they've had a lot of comfort in that. And I know some people have found it hard to be on medication and have that taken away. It can be really complicated.

I can vouch for this. I hear voices, but how they talk to me depends on my mood. I have bipolar, and the voice I hear when I'm in a manic, elevated mood is encouraging. They make me laugh and motivate me to do new things or finish a difficult job. I even have my own inside jokes with the voice I hear when I'm manic. You could even say they're a friend. When I'm stable, I honestly miss having them around because they would give me an extra boost of confidence each day. I've missed them so much that I've sometimes contemplated not taking my medication in the hope it would trigger a manic episode and the voice. I'll make it clear: I'm not endorsing not taking medication if you're prescribed it. If you're unhappy about any medication you're taking, talk to a medical professional about alternatives – if you feel that will work for you.

Now it's time to move on to the top three.

People with psychosis are always ill and should be in a hospital

What image first comes to mind when someone says 'psychosis' or 'psychotic'? For many people, it's a person in a strait jacket, rocking back and forth in a padded cell in a hospital. A person drugged, sedated, and thrown into a locked room with no hope of recovery or chance to participate in society. A person so out of touch with reality they can never recover, doomed to be locked away for the rest of their life. This isn't true, but a myth that's repeated over and over again. If people see and hear the same myth and never see or hear about the reality, of course, it will become the truth for many.

It's easy to forget that real people are psychotic and live regular lives, and they're not a caricature in a strait jacket. Sara is not defined by the psychosis she experiences and wants people to understand there's more to her life and identity.

Another misconception that people think when they hear 'psychosis' is that you can't live a fulfilling life; you should be hospitalized and drugged. And that's it. That's all you are. And as bad as it can be, sometimes it's not always bad. And I think people miss that a lot. We have personalities and things about us. We're not just a diagnosis.

Human beings are multifaceted and complicated, and we can be a bit messy – that's how we all are. We're all guilty of boiling someone down in the most simplistic ways:

- They're horrible, awful, a really nasty person. I can't stand them.
- They're boring. There's nothing interesting about them.
- They're psychotic; they should be locked away in a hospital.

We should all try to be better; how we judge others is part of that process – getting to know someone behind our initial judgement and realizing that they're just as contradictory, confused, passionate, vibrant, and alive as we are!

If you experience psychosis, it's not 'on' all the time. It's not activated, and then that's it. Most people refer to 'episodes of psychosis' because that's how it manifests. For Jen, her experience was temporary.

> People think you're mad, all the time. When really, for me, it was a very brief episode. So, it doesn't last forever. It's just a brief episode for some people. So, some people think you're psychotic all the time, but it was just very brief in my case.

For some people, it's like a conveyor belt: after the off button has been pressed, it takes a while to slow down and finally come to a halt.

In some situations, it starts as if you've entered an app on your phone, and it's there instantly. As soon as that app is closed, it's gone as instantly as it began.

Some episodes of psychosis last longer than others. I've experienced fleeting hallucinations that have lasted less than an hour. I've also experienced longer delusions that lasted months. Both ended, and with both, I didn't need to be hospitalized. The reason I didn't need to have a stay in hospital was because of my support network: my partner, family, friends, and my mental health team who took care of me so I could stay in the community.

People with psychosis can't function in society

This one's difficult to pick apart. It's really about drilling down to what that person means when they say 'functioning'. And that all depends on someone's upbringing and role models, worldview, spirituality, or religion – anything that makes up their personality. They could be telling you:

- You're not functioning if you can't hold down a full-time job.

- You're not functioning if you're unemployed and unable to work.
- You're not functioning if you're claiming benefits.
- You're not functioning if you can't keep on top of bills and life admin without help.
- You're not functioning if you find parties and big social groups too overwhelming.

On top of this, the assumption is that if you live with psychosis, you'll never be able to function in society; everyone experiencing psychosis is in the same boat, and you're constantly unwell. Because of this, many people still believe that if you have psychosis, you should be 'locked away' in a mental health hospital and not given a chance to be part of society.

For some people, psychosis is a linear experience. It might be a one-off psychotic episode, or they find an effective treatment. For others, it's a lifelong journey of managing psychosis, often alongside a mental illness. To say 'people with psychosis can't function in society' is a massive generalization to make because it affects one person very differently from another. Sara was diagnosed with schizophrenia and works full-time. She told me it's hard to hear this myth when she tells someone about her diagnosis.

I have a full-time job, and sometimes I'll tell people about my condition. And they'll be like, 'Oh, well, I didn't think people with your condition worked. I didn't think that people with your condition could function.' And I'm like, well, it's different for everyone. There are different severities of it. And everyone's got a different experience. But I feel when people say you can't live a life, it feels really horrible. Their assumption about your reality is that you just can't live life.

It's true that not everyone with psychosis can work full-time. I'm one of those people. I spent way too many years pretending I was fine with working 30- or 40-hour-plus weeks in a high-pressure job, then having a psychotic episode when the stress had built to a crescendo. I feel like going back in time and telling myself, 'Get the hint, Kai!' It wasn't healthy. Now I'm firmer with the part of me that thinks, 'Life would be easier if I earned more money.' On a surface level, yes, it would. But I know the stress and pressure would again overwhelm me, and I'd have to resign anyway – and that's exactly how the cycle begins! I work for myself as a freelance writer now, and it's manageable most of the time – even if my boss is a nightmare, and the Xmas party is just me dancing around the cat and my partner looking bemused. There have also been times when I've been unemployed, and I found ways to bring value and meaning to my life through my connections with friends, looking after my young niece once a week, and volunteering.

CHANGING THE FOCUS OF WHAT 'FUNCTIONING' MEANS

An argument can be made that our modern capitalist society, as it is now, doesn't value alternative ways to function, participate, or contribute to society. If you're not paying into the economy by working a job, you're not a valuable member of society.

We're raised on this idea. We're told absences from school are always negative – even if you're living with a disability, and that includes mental illness. Even in research and studies focusing on severe mental illness, I've seen the figures highlighted for how much money is 'lost' to mental ill health and absences. Mental health services are often geared towards getting you back to work and finding employment rather than exploring alternatives. Life should be fulfilling, and your worth and value not solely focused on your ability to work.

Sam explains that people like her want to be part of society and be involved in their local community, but those opportunities are rare for many people.

> I think the way society functions means that people with psychosis are forgotten. I think there must be a misconception that people with psychotic illnesses don't want to take part in society, as there are few things to engage with if you don't live in a big city. Only 8 per cent of people with psychosis in the UK are in work without any disability benefits [Royal College of Psychiatrists 2021], and different studies show only 5–15 per cent in work at all, but there's very little for us to do during the day. I think this is a consequence of society not seeing that people with serious mental illness have social needs to be part of the community. And also because capitalism dominates everything. We need to be more compassionate as a society.

When society revolves around work, it does sometimes feel that if you have psychosis, you're overlooked. It's not enough to keep yourself well; people need support in the community, and they need places to go where they can meet other people and actively engage in activities. Feeling isolated and forgotten will make people vulnerable and more likely to fall into a crisis where they can't look after themselves.

Contributing, functioning – or whatever you want to call it – is interpreted in various ways. It's not straightforward, and the waters get murkier when you throw something like psychosis into the mix. Libby neatly summed it up.

> I think it's hard because everyone has this idea of what contributing to society looks like. And I think it's not as black and white as a lot of people think it is. Because literally, just having

connections with other people is contributing to society. You don't have to be changing the world. You can just be making a difference in one person's life. And I think that's enough. You don't even have to do that. Just making a difference in your own life. That is enough.

People with psychosis are dangerous

You'll remember from Chapter 1 that the idea that people with psychosis are dangerous has cropped up already. With most of the people I interviewed, it seemed at the forefront of their minds when stigma and psychosis were mentioned. In each interview, it was mentioned at least once. It's a prevalent myth that damages people's views of psychosis. It's a way of 'othering' people with psychosis – that they're violent, scary, and unpredictable.

It's a way for the general public to detach themselves from something they don't understand by labelling those that experience psychosis as dangerous. Best to leave them alone, keep your distance, and don't engage with anyone with psychosis. People can wash their hands of it to keep themselves safe.

Hazel and I spoke about how, unless they know someone personally, the general public only witnesses a specific version of psychosis.

> It's almost like there's two types of psychosis. There's the loud, shouty one which everyone knows about, and then there's the quiet 'hides away in a house and slowly starves to death' one that no one notices. But they're both relevant, and they're both as serious as each other. But we only hear about the loud, shouty, 'running down the street' one.

However psychosis manifests, the living, breathing person

behind the illness is extremely unwell and needs help to get better. Most of us have come across someone on public transport or as we walk around our town or city who's agitated. They might be shouting or acting strangely, but they almost always appear distressed. It makes us uncomfortable, and if you're on your own, that behaviour can feel scary and threatening. What is missed when we talk to friends and other people about these random encounters is that someone in this state is much more likely to be a danger to themselves than to others. It's also a tiny fraction of a massive spectrum of experiences and behaviours that manifest when someone is psychotic. It's easy to forget there's a person behind psychosis who, later, when they're feeling better, will probably be embarrassed, ashamed, or deeply upset by their behaviour.

Sam feels the film industry plays a large part in perpetuating the myth everyone with psychosis is dangerous.

> People often wrongly associate psychosis with being a violent serial killer because of the film industry, but people with psychosis are more likely to be victims than perpetrators.

With all that in mind, society generally doesn't feel responsible for keeping people with psychosis safe, taking responsibility for keeping them well, or showing empathy or compassion. What isn't focused on is the reality: that someone going through psychosis is very poorly and extremely vulnerable.

It isn't just anecdotal evidence and individuals' experiences that say this is true, but peer-reviewed scientific studies and analysis. Numerous studies have shown that those with a psychotic disorder are more likely to be the victims of crime and violence than the perpetrators.

According to de Vries and colleagues (2019), 'Victimization

rates were approximately 4–6 times higher than in the general community [...] Depending on the examined time period, 1 in 5 (assessment period ≤3 y) or 1 in 3 (assessment period entire adulthood) people with a psychotic disorder were victim of a crime.'

When we talk about crime, it means both:

- non-violent crimes without physical contact including threats, burglary, theft of money or property, identity theft, and fraud

and

- violent crimes including being threatened with a weapon, mugging, robbery, assault, rape, and sexual harassment.

As I explained in Chapter 1, psychosis is a symptom of a number of severe mental illnesses. Studies have shown there's a link between living with a severe mental illness and being a victim of crime and violence.

According to Khalifeh and colleagues (2016):

Women with SMI (severe mental illness) had four-, ten- and four-fold increases in the odds of experiencing domestic, community and sexual violence, respectively. Victims with SMI were more likely to report psychosocial morbidity following violence than victims from the general population. People with SMI are at greatly increased risk of crime and associated morbidity. Violence prevention policies should be particularly focused on people with SMI.

Being a victim of crime has a lasting impact, especially for those with a psychotic illness. Psychosocial morbidity in this study refers to how people with severe mental illness struggle to cope socially, physically, and mentally after being victims of violence. It's vital that we speak about how people of colour with psychosis are at an increased risk of being victims of crime, and the higher rates that black people with psychosis are detained and arrested by police. In Part II, I'll look at this in more detail.

Why are people with psychosis more at risk of being victims of crime and violence?

Think for a minute about what it means to be in a psychotic episode.

- You've lost touch with reality and can't decipher if what you believe is a delusion or what you're seeing, hearing, or sensing is real or a hallucination.
- You might feel intensely paranoid, unsafe around other people, and extremely cautious of real or imaginary threats.
- You might have problems communicating what you need or expressing what's happening to you.
- You might believe that you don't need help from anyone or you're the most important person in the world.

In all of these states, there's one common thread: it makes you vulnerable to people who want to take advantage of you. Psychosis can make you an easy target; unfortunately, some people will see this as an opportunity. Psychosis might also manifest in a way that makes people angry or hostile toward you. You might appear agitated, or you might be acting in a way that's unusual or strange. You might say the wrong thing to the wrong person, or someone might take offence at your behaviour. People with psychosis are more likely to be unemployed, have an insecure living situation, live in an area with a higher crime rate, or lack a steady support network, which all contribute to a higher risk of being a victim of crime.

How do you explain to other people that psychosis doesn't automatically make you dangerous?

Michelle has found a unique way to explain what a psychotic episode looks like for her, by showing her followers on Instagram and TikTok.

> I share videos of myself with my security cam of me and these psychotic episodes, while sitting on my couch watching TV. Now, does that seem dangerous? So the whole point is: there you go – a psychosis episode. I'm watching TV, but not watching TV. But it was my plan to watch TV. But then I have to rewind, of course. But that's the whole thing. I'm trying to show people. No, there's an episode right there. Nobody's getting injured. Nobody's getting hurt. Nobody's running around nuts, just trying to hurt people. So that's a huge misconception that there's danger involved. There can be absolutely no danger. It's just a word.

Chris has his own way of explaining why psychosis doesn't make him dangerous, and it makes a point about how crime and violence can be committed by anyone.

> I would just say to someone that you're just as capable as me. Like we're mammals. And don't forget that. People try to forget that part of it, the id. When someone says something like that to me, it's either you walk away and just don't give them attention. Or if I do say something, it's hard because I've had to hold my

friggin' breath before I even answer because the kinds of things that people ask you can be really ridiculous, or the boxes they shove you in can be very harmful.

People going through psychosis sometimes break the law. It happens, and when incidents happen, they often make the news. It skews our opinion of what psychosis looks like and what someone having a psychotic episode is capable of; in other words, we believe what the news tells us – that psychosis always makes people violent and dangerous.

Sara reflects on news stories she's seen on TV or read about in the media and how they mould people's views and opinions about psychosis.

I ask them (when told people with psychosis are dangerous) to evaluate why they think those things. I think often it's because they've listened to news broadcasts that talk about where, 'Oh, somebody with schizophrenia has thrown somebody on to a railway line.' So, they'll look at that and think that must be what everyone with that diagnosis does, even though violence and stuff like that are not at all linked to those illnesses. It's a very, very, very small percentage. Most people who commit those sorts of acts don't have mental health problems. I think people miss that a lot.

Jen, who made threats when she was experiencing an intense paranoid delusion during her first and only major psychotic episode, talked me through how she explains the experience to others.

I just say no, I'm not. It was just a brief episode. Once I was on medication, I was completely sane. And the medication kicks in quite quickly, to be honest. So, it was just a brief, random, completely out-of-the-blue episode in my life. Because a lot of people associate psychosis with schizophrenia, and they think, well, that's something you'll have for life. Psychosis covers a whole range of people's experiences.

How to myth-bust in the real world

Psychosis is still very misunderstood. When we feel able to, we should try to break down these misconceptions and demystify psychosis. The longer the general public sees psychosis as shrouded in mystery, the longer these false beliefs and opinions will stick around. The problem with myths and misconceptions is if you hold them, you already think you're right. You believe you have all the proper information. You won't go out of your way to read up on psychosis or ask questions because you think you already have all the answers!

While planning this book, I was constantly thinking about how this information can be used in people's daily lives and conversations to tackle all the misinformation out there about psychosis. Getting your point across is hard, especially when you feel something that you live with is up for debate.

So, I've put together some quick answers that get straight to the point to counteract any misconceptions you hear in your daily life.

Each question has two different answers. Why? It comes down to your experience of psychosis and how you want to answer each question.

Answer one is for those of you who know someone with psychosis, but you haven't experienced it yourself. It's also for those of us with psychosis, but when we don't want to bring our lived experience into the discussion. We might not know the person we're speaking to very well or they're someone in our life we haven't been open with about our experiences. It's also a way of keeping ourselves safe when we feel fragile or vulnerable or from a conversation that could turn confrontational.

Answer two is for those conversations where we feel our lived experience will impact their point of view. Lived experience is a valuable tool. It helps someone put a face to the idea of psychosis, where they may have only ever had a vague impression of a mad, scary person before – not a friend, colleague, or acquaintance in front of them speaking calmly and rationally about their experience.

If you don't have psychosis but want to speak on behalf of someone who does, I'd stick to **answer one**. Using someone else's experiences of psychosis to make a point makes for a powerful argument, and it might feel like the right thing to do, but I would be cautious of it. They might feel uncomfortable with their experiences being used in that way or may have told you in confidence. Psychosis is complicated, and you may have missed some subtleties of their experiences, or you might not fully understand what they went through. However, if you have permission to share someone's experiences and feel the circumstances are right, then go for it.

'People with psychosis are dangerous.'

A1: 'People with psychosis are much more likely to be victims of violence or crime than to commit them. There is no direct correlation between psychosis and violence or crime.'

A2: 'I have psychosis; I'm at a higher risk of being a victim of violence or crime when I'm unwell. It makes me more vulnerable to people that want to take advantage of me.'

'You can't function in society if you have psychosis.'

A1: 'Psychosis affects everyone differently, but people with psychosis can function outside a hospital and contribute to society – they have jobs, hobbies, friendships, and relationships.'

A2: 'When I'm supported, have effective treatment, and look after my wellbeing, I can contribute to society – in my own way.'

'You should be in hospital if you have psychosis.'

A1: 'Psychosis can be managed in and out of the hospital; some people find hospital stays damaging and traumatizing. Someone with psychosis doesn't need to be locked away forever. Psychosis is episodic; they're not constantly ill.'

A2: 'I have psychosis, and I don't need to be hospitalized for the rest of my life or even every time I'm unwell. I don't experience psychosis constantly. If I receive help and treatment early on in a psychotic episode, I can stay at home with support.'

'I could never understand what it's like to have psychosis.'

A1: 'If you think about it, we all have experiences we can't explain. We hear or see something strange when we're half-awake or have a dream we wake up from and are convinced it was real.'

A2: 'When I'm in psychosis, I perceive reality differently compared with when I'm well. It's much more intense and overwhelming than something you might have experienced, but it can give you a glimpse of what I go through.'

'Psychosis only happens to teenagers and young people.'

A1: 'It usually happens to people between the ages of 15 and 30, but there are things other than a severe mental illness that can cause psychosis.'

A2: 'I first experienced a psychotic episode when I was xx years old, but it's different for everyone.'

'People pretend to have psychosis and use it as an excuse to get out of trouble.'

A1: 'It's very difficult to fake an episode of psychosis. It's not the same as how it's portrayed on television and in film. You would still have to face the consequences if you committed a crime.'

A2: 'I don't think someone who hasn't experienced psychosis could pretend for very long. You can't fake it. When I'm unwell, it's obvious that I'm not thinking rationally, and the things I say don't make any sense.'

'Psychosis means you're not capable of understanding difficult concepts or holding a conversation.'

A1: 'Psychosis doesn't make people less intelligent. They might struggle during a psychotic episode to communicate or concentrate, but when they're well, they're as capable as anyone else.'

A2: 'When I'm unwell, I find it difficult to take care of myself, and it might appear that I'm struggling to understand the world around me. When I'm well, I can be articulate and participate in conversations. I'm capable and can study, work, or pursue creative interests.'

'You only hear nasty and negative things; it's never positive.'

A1: 'Psychosis affects each person differently. Some do have positive experiences.'

A2: (Include your own positive experiences, if you have any.)

'Psychosis is just like having multiple personalities.'

A1: 'Multiple personalities are a symptom of dissociative identity disorder (DID), not psychosis.'

A2: 'Psychosis affects how I see, hear, or feel things and what I believe is real. It doesn't change me or give me multiple personalities.'

At the end of this book, I'll share resources to which you can signpost people if they want more information or clarification that what you're telling them is true, or if they would like to do further reading on their own. Plus, all the research and studies cited throughout the book are available online if they want the full picture!

Myths and misconceptions won't disappear overnight; let's be honest here – they'll probably be around for the foreseeable future. Even if you only manage to change one person's point of view, that's enough. Or even, for instance, make someone question and reflect on why they believe all people with psychosis should be forever hospitalized. It will have a ripple effect: they might treat someone with psychosis positively, or they might educate others in their day-to-day conversations. Neither of these is a grand gesture or likely to change the world, but both actions will ripple out to the edges of their own pool of people and connections that make up their life.

If you've experienced psychosis, you can make a difference by being yourself. It isn't your duty to go out there and confront every person spreading harmful myths about psychosis. I've been battling against these misconceptions and stigma since 2012, and it's really tough to keep going and stay motivated. I mean *really* tough. Unless you're bulletproof, you can't challenge everything negative you hear. You can let people know what you've experienced and then continue to be who you are. Don't change the way you act around people who know your experience. Show them who you are, and they'll see that psychosis doesn't make a person unrelatable, incapable, or dangerous because they know you and enjoy your company. That is enough.

Chapter 3
Delusions

In these next two chapters, we'll look at delusions and hallucinations and really breaking down what psychosis is. This book is all about stigma and how it has a massive impact on people who live with psychosis. The first step to breaking down stigma is education. If people don't understand what psychosis is, if they don't understand the ins and outs of what it's like to face it, then they can never truly connect and empathize with those of us who experience psychosis. People will continue to stigmatize those who experience hallucinations and delusions if they have limited knowledge and access to lived-experience stories. These next few chapters are all about those stories. Each person I've interviewed has had at least one experience of psychosis. Some deal with it every day, and some have lifelong conditions that are connected to psychotic episodes. For others, it's a rare experience. I'll also be talking about some of my own experiences and sharing some of the journal entries I kept during those times.

We'll be focusing on:

- the difference between hallucinations and delusions

- how it's not as simple as only a hallucination or just a delusion
- the distinct types of hallucinations, from hearing voices to seeing strange optical illusions
- the several types of delusions, from delusions of grandeur to paranoid delusions.

Every experience is unique, and each individual has their own approach to handling psychosis. They all have differing views about how it affects their lives. Some people feel it's an extremely negative experience to go through, whereas others have a mixed view of the psychosis experience. And some will find it an incredibly positive experience.

So, let's get started.

Psychosis is different for everyone. Yes, I know, I've already said it, and I'll keep saying it because it really needs to be emphasized. If you have someone in your life who has had a psychotic episode, ask them about it because *it will be different for them from all the stories you hear in this book*. You might be thinking, 'Well, what's the point of reading this book then, Kai?!' Yes, their story will be different, but it's a way of connecting with that person by saying, 'I read this book about psychosis...what's your experience like?' They may identify with some of the points made in the book and some of the stories told, but theirs will be different and unique to them. It's the same if you've experienced psychosis. We have our own stories to tell of hallucinations and delusions, and it can be easy to become wrapped up in our own experience and not consider others. Reading about other experiences can show us how different psychotic episodes can be, but how they're still relatable regardless of your own experience. I'm hoping the stories told in this book will resonate and make you feel less isolated and know you're not alone.

Psychosis can be incredibly upsetting and distressing. It can be strange and bizarre, to the point that it can almost make you laugh, and even laugh out loud. It's happened to me, but that's a story for later. It can be positive, and sometimes people will find it is a quite transformative experience. Some people find the voices they hear are almost like friends, so it's completely different. It's such a vast array of experiences, and I think that reflects the human experience and how we all differ so much from each other.

What's the difference between hallucinations and delusions?

Hallucinations are about hearing, seeing, or feeling things that aren't actually there. A hallucination is a distorted view of your sensory experience. It's a sensory phenomenon and is characterized by perception in the absence of sensory stimulus. In other words, you're perceiving something with one or more of your senses without a real source that you or anyone else can identify. Some people may only experience hearing voices, while others encounter a range of hallucinations.

Delusions are more about a distorted view of your reality in general. Delusions are about how you perceive the world rather than how your senses are perceiving the world.

A common experience is when someone has a psychotic episode, and these two experiences merge, so hallucinations and delusions are experienced as part of one episode. This might, be for example, someone who's paranoid and they believe the government is spying on them. They might start hearing voices talking and discussing them. They might start seeing things that aren't actually there, but still feel that delusional belief.

I'll share something with you now. As I'm writing this book, I've just emerged from a very serious psychotic episode. I'm not sure if it was the interviews I conducted for this book that reminded me of my own psychotic episodes, or if it was the stress from my personal life that I was under, or the lack of sleep which led to the soul-crushing insomnia I experienced. But something triggered it. It all started with a feeling when I picked up my phone, picked up my laptop, touched a light switch or an electrical cable, or put a plug in an electrical socket – I felt through my fingers, hands, and my wrists that I was having waves of short, sharp electric shocks that caused pain. When I put down my phone or stopped touching anything electrical, the feeling would go away. The pain would disappear. I knew it wasn't real, that it wasn't a thing, but it was probably, like, 99 per cent psychosis. I think because I knew it wasn't realistic and it was all in my head, there was a part of me thinking, 'Well, why do I still feel this way? Why am I still having these electric shocks in my hands? Why is it still happening even though I know, logically, it doesn't make sense.' I started thinking, 'Maybe it is real.'

Then it escalated. What happened next was I started to physically feel that my internal organs were rotting. I believed I was decaying from the inside out. It made me feel hair was falling out. When I tried to exercise and sweated, it made me feel like the sweat was a by-product of my decaying insides. This combination meant I couldn't eat because I thought, 'Well, what's the point?' Why would you eat if you were already rotting inside? As you can imagine, it was an incredibly intense, distressing feeling, and my mood plummeted. I wasn't sure what would happen – if I was dying – but I knew how I felt and I truly believed this was happening to my body. It felt so visceral, almost as though I could feel something changing inside my body. Again, I knew logically this didn't make sense, and I'm a very logical person, but I couldn't think my way out of it.

That's an important note to make about delusions. You can't think your way around them; you can't think your way through them. They're your reality until they aren't. Sometimes a delusion goes on its own. It figures itself out. Usually, though, you need intervention from medical professionals or a therapist. That's what I needed, and I ended up speaking to my psychiatrist (organized by my partner Jimi, as I was too unwell to contact the local mental health team) and we came up with a plan. The number-one problem was sleep, and as soon as that was sorted, and I was sleeping more than two hours a night, the delusions started to dissipate. Then one day, they completely disappeared.

So that's just one example from me of something that started out as a weird tactile hallucination which quickly shifted into an intense delusion. I had that mental health crisis, got support, and quickly received the help I needed. I felt better and started writing this book!

I've learned that psychosis is just something that happens to me, however silly that sounds. It's something that does crop up, and I look at it as almost a way my mind is telling me something isn't right. 'You're not OK, you're not looking after yourself. You're stressed out. You're not sleeping.' It usually means I've not been looking after myself; I've not been listening to my body or what it needs. For me, it's also something that happens, and it can be quite disabling, but when it's over, I'm able to function and capable of looking after myself. I call them 'blips' and then I'm fine again – whatever that means because I think my 'fine' is very different to other people's!

The many types of delusions

So, I've spoken about my own experience of delusions, but now let's consider what they look like for different people. I briefly touched on this in the first chapter, but we're going to go into more detail now. Put simply, delusions are when you believe something that is not true. Now that's an incredibly simplistic way of explaining it, but that's what it is! With that in mind, we're going to break it down further and look at the different ways delusions manifest.

Delusions can be based on real events, of things that could technically happen but are extremely unlikely. Delusions can also be anything but realistic and can be strange and bizarre experiences.

SOMATIC DELUSIONS

What I've just described from my own recent experience would be classified as somatic. This type of delusion is focused on physical sensations and beliefs on and in your body.

You might believe something is physically wrong with your body, and a somatic delusion may focus on illnesses and real-life conditions:

- believing you have cancer
- feeling that you're pregnant even if it's technically impossible.

Somatic delusions can also be bizarre:

- believing your bones are twisting inside your body
- feeling something is wrong with your internal organs, or some of them are missing.

You're likely to want to try to find the source of the problem, so start to make regular visits to a doctor or hospital and ask for medical tests even though there is nothing physically wrong with you. Despite negative results, you'll still believe there's something wrong with your body.

DELUSIONS OF REFERENCE

It's the belief that everything happening around you is connected when it isn't. They're sometimes called ideas of reference, but some sources, clinicians, and researchers will use the term 'delusions of reference' to describe an episode which has a significant impact on a person's life.

We've all felt that all eyes are on us when we're walking down the street, or we've believed everyone is talking about us at a party. But it's fleeting; it quickly passes and you can get on with your day or enjoy the party.

When this feeling happens constantly, or you feel complete strangers are whispering, talking, or laughing at you and about you, it might be a problem. When it gets to the point where you feel the need to hide and can't leave your home, then it's more than likely a delusion.

Sam explained to me her experiences with delusions of reference.

My main experience during psychosis is that people are out to get me. Who it is constantly changes based on what I see, because I have delusions of reference and interpret meaning from things, which then changes the conspiracies. To name just a few, I've thought that Extinction Rebellion, the police, Derren Brown, the government, my old co-workers, my friends, my family, friends I've lost touch with, the whole of society, a group of serial killers, a group of journalists, neighbours, were out to get me.

GRANDIOSE DELUSIONS

Sometimes called delusions of grandeur, it's an outlandish belief – something that could never possibly happen, that's outside the physical laws of nature or the laws of physics. It could be something fantastical, or it could be you believe you're somebody else or in a position you could never possibly hold. Grandiose delusions are common in people who have psychosis-related disorders. They affect two-thirds of people with bipolar disorder and half of people with schizophrenia (Isham et al. 2019) Examples include:

- believing you're in a position of power, famous, or fabulously wealthy
- believing you're some form of deity, God, or spiritual leader
- believing you're all-powerful, invincible, or impervious to harm
- believing you've discovered a new scientific theory, such as the cure for cancer, or a way of thinking that doesn't make sense to anybody else, such as believing unlocking the secret to time travel is as simple as barrel rolling down a hill.

Libby has experienced grandiose delusions, where she truly believed she'd found a miracle cure.

I thought at one point I found the cure to cancer. I thought it was mayonnaise, which I laugh about now. I actually wrote a diary entry which is talking about how I can't believe I found the cure for cancer and it's in everyone's cupboards and I was convinced the government were sending people to kill me because I found the cure for cancer. A big conspiracy.

Grandiose delusions give you self-worth, confidence, and a sense of belonging. The downside is these delusions can lead to risk taking and behaviour that's dangerous and could put you in harm's way.

When I'm manic, I experience delusions. I think I can do anything. I have what's called delusions of grandeur, where I believe I'm better than everyone else. I will think that I can do no wrong, and I'm always the smartest person in the room. Actually, it's more than that. I'll truly believe that only I have all the answers, and I'm the smartest person that ever existed. This type of thinking causes me to react to people irrationally and often aggressively.

'How dare they think they're better than me!' I will say to myself.

'How can they possibly question me when I have all the answers!'

'Everyone around me is ignorant and stupid. They should all listen to me.'

What mania makes me is incredibly confident. Sometimes this confidence turns into delusion. I believe everything I am creating is like gold dust and must be seen and shared. I have written reams and reams of notes of ideas for a book, at the time believing them to be the best ideas I've ever had. When I look back on them later, all I see is scribbled nonsense, a stream of consciousness, misspelled, and a jumble of words. It's as though the pages of these notebooks are a reflection of my manic mind. My mind is constantly darting from one idea to another and never finishing my original point. My mind is distracted by the smallest spark of an idea, and every thought that comes to mind grips my attention. I show everyone what I've been working on, with a pride that verges on narcissism.

Other times when I'm manic, the delusions I encounter put me in danger. A recurring belief is that I can stop traffic. I believe if I step into a road, every car, bus, and lorry will immediately stop, and I can walk safely across. I also think that even if this power becomes faulty in some way, I will not be hurt.

I don't believe there is some greater power watching over me, but instead I'm so important I have become invincible. I live in a busy town with its fair share of traffic, so you can imagine the danger I have put myself in. I've had many near misses as I've walked along busy roads and have stepped out with no fear and no thought for the repercussions. I've been hit by vehicles twice and had a near miss with a double-decker bus. On both occasions of being knocked over, I was extremely lucky not to be seriously hurt and came away with just a few cuts and bruises. Unfortunately, not being hurt on both occasions fuelled my belief that I was invincible.

PERSECUTORY DELUSIONS

Also known as paranoid delusions, these are a form of delusion when you have the feeling you're being watched. This can escalate to believing people want to hurt you, believing your food has been poisoned, or feeling as though there's a foreign object inside you that shouldn't be there, such as a parasite.

Jen told me about a paranoid delusion she experienced which completely took over her life.

I guess the biggest delusion I had was when I thought somebody had drugged my food with tapeworm eggs. And I thought I had a parasite in my brain that was slowly killing me. And I went to doctor after doctor, to my GP saying, 'I need a brain scan, I need a brain scan.' And they were all telling me, 'You don't have a parasite in your brain. If you did, you would have physical symptoms.' And I thought it was slowly killing me. And I was getting worse and worse and worse. And then I went to the restaurant where I had the food and said, 'I know you did this', and I made threats. And that's when I was arrested; it just got gradually more and more out of hand.

I asked Jen how it felt when she believed no one was listening to her, and what it was like to feel so distressed.

> I was very concerned that it was slowly killing me. Because you can get a parasite in your head – it's very rare, but you can. I was convinced this had happened to me. And I was just so worried about dying that I went to the extreme and made threats.

Persecutory delusions can also lead to believing some great conspiracy is happening. They're often referred to as an extreme form of paranoia and may present alongside other symptoms such as:

- anxiety
- difficulty sleeping
- negative thoughts about yourself
- depression.

Persecutory or paranoid delusions are the most common form of delusions, but they manifest in a plethora of different ways. This became obvious during my interviews, as well as how debilitating, confusing, and scary paranoid delusions can be.

Sara's paranoid delusions were more fixated on being spied on, and she explained to me what it felt like to experience them.

> I think a common one for me is the belief that the government and authorities are spying on me. That's been a prominent one. I mean, I've had this for about four or five years now, and that seems to be one of the prominent things that I've experienced the stress with, and I think it can translate in hallucinations, as well as delusions. So I might see people following me or cameras, and one that I had was I'm seeing cameras flashing from

my attic. Obviously, I was on my own, and so I couldn't work it out. In that moment, you just don't understand what's going on.

I asked Sara if paranoid delusions were like a fixation and something you just couldn't move on from.

> You're just trying to understand what's going on! But sometimes you end up just getting farther and farther into the delusion. And you end up making it worse. It's like, 'Why am I doing this? What is going on?'

Sara explained how these delusions are not connected to anything in your life.

> It's just completely out of everything else. And you're like, 'What relevance does this have?' It's confusing.

Sam explained how in some ways her delusions make her a better person, but quickly escalate into something scary and intrusive.

> One of my main delusions is actually that Extinction Rebellion are out to get me. This affects so much of my life. I want to eat healthier, buy fresh fruit and be vegan, try to give up smoking, I pick up rubbish from the ground. It sounds almost good for me, but it's terrifying. I think I'm going to be killed and maimed. I think when I say this, people think I am against Extinction Rebellion, but I believe we should work together to save the planet. I'm not sure there's that much rhyme or reason to my delusions; they seem to be inflamed by the way things are covered in the media. I see disposable coffee cups and think they have been put there to remind me that I am an awful person

who is singularly responsible for global warming. It sounds harmless, but honestly, it affects almost every facet of my life and the feeling that goes with it is that I will be maimed or killed.

DELUSIONS OF CONTROL

With this type of delusion, you believe someone or a group of people are trying to control your thoughts and behaviours. I'll say here that many of these types of delusions feed into each other. If you believe you're being controlled, then you'll probably start to become extremely paranoid, which is where persecutory delusions come in.

Libby's delusions of control stemmed from a real-life experience of losing a friend to suicide.

So about two, three years ago, my best friend had died in the April. I stopped taking my medication and became convinced that her mental health team had given up on her for the last six months of her life. I became convinced that they were trying to frame me for her suicide, which I laugh about now. It's not funny, though. So I stopped seeing them. My CPN [community psychiatric nurse] would turn up at my door and I'd be like, 'Oh, no, I can't see you today.' I was not seeing anyone. I thought that he had bugged the living room. So I didn't leave my bedroom. I stopped talking to friends. It went on for about three, four months. I can't really remember how I got out of it. I know I started taking my medication, but I can't remember why. I can't remember what happened. It's completely blank. But that was really difficult at the time. I had different things happen during that time. So different small things that I don't know if they were delusions, but I guess they were, but they didn't last long. Like mini, fleeting delusions.

JEALOUS DELUSIONS

You'll begin to believe your partner is being unfaithful, without a shred of evidence to back up your belief. You'll constantly be looking for evidence of their infidelity and misinterpret innocent behaviour from your partner.

EROTOMANIC DELUSIONS

Erotomanic delusions are when you believe another person is in love with you, when they're not. It might be someone you've never met, like a celebrity. It goes beyond a crush, and you might start to believe you are in contact with them or they're sending you secret messages.

MIXED OR UNSPECIFIED DELUSIONS

Sometimes delusions don't fit into a specific category. Many of these types are not set in stone, so the category 'mixed or unspecified' is when you experience multiple types of delusions, but there isn't one type that stands out or happens more often than the rest.

Delusions vary wildly, so they're also categorized by a theme. Some of them are self-explanatory or are very similar to categories we've already covered, but I'll fill in the gaps.

- Persecution – a similar theme to persecutory or paranoid delusions.
- Negation/nihilistic – this is the belief that something or someone no longer exists. You might start to believe that you're dead or parts of your body are missing. You may even believe the world has ceased to exist. This type of delusion is rare and is often linked to severe and chronic depression.

- Infidelity – very similar to jealous delusions.
- Love – very similar to erotomanic delusions.
- Religion – you'll begin to believe that you have supernatural, God-like powers, or you are actually God. You may hear or believe God is speaking to you directly and asking you to carry out their wishes. This delusion makes you feel important and can be linked to a lack of self-esteem.
- Guilt/unworthiness – you'll believe that you've ruined your loved one's lives and you're an evil, terrible person. The belief that you've committed an awful crime or sin will be so strong that you'll feel you deserve to be punished for the rest of your life and beyond. This delusion is accompanied by low self-esteem and severe depression.

Chapter 4
Hallucinations

Now it's time to take a closer look at hallucinations. We'll be going through each type of hallucination as we did with delusions. I'll be sharing the experiences of Chris, Sara, Libby, Kody, and Michelle, and how hallucinations impact their lives. I'll also be sharing my own experiences of hearing voices. As with delusions, some hallucinations are more common than others, so let's start with those first.

Auditory hallucinations

This type is one of the most common hallucinations, but it manifests differently from person to person. Put simply, auditory hallucinations are when you hear something when there is no sound to hear, you're the only person who can hear the noise, or you hear a variety of sounds and voices all of which are not real.

- You might hear sounds like someone walking around, such as in the room above you, behind you, or all around.

- You might hear repetitive noises like clicking or tapping.
- You may hear a single voice, such as a person speaking directly to you, or numerous voices chattering but not necessarily talking to you.
- A voice you hear might tell you to do things or to harm yourself.
- Voices can be angry, confrontational, or negative.
- Voices can be neutral.
- Voices can be friendly, comforting, and positive.

I asked Hazel which voice was the most common they heard.

> I mean, it would probably be Nigel because he is consistent. And even on medication, I can still hear him. He just never, never goes away! There are other voices I hear, and they bugger off when I'm on meds, but he is just there. He reinforces any delusions, he reinforces paranoia. He commands me to do things, he comments on everything around me. So, he's just...just there.
>
> When I'm not very ill, he's just like a narrator. When I'm more ill, the only way I can think of to describe it is I'm secretly a spy. And he's my handler talking to me in my ear. So, it'll be information plus telling me what to do plus passing comment on how I'm doing.

Many people with psychosis give names to their voices. As for me, I call them Gremlins, because often they're overlapping voices who chatter incessantly. Sometimes they make sense, sometimes it's like a wall of noise, or beads of water on a wall, and each voice is the trickle of water sliding slowly downwards. I also hear what I call the Chaos Gremlin. More about them later. I asked Hazel why they gave a name to the voice they hear most often,

I gave him the name a couple of years ago. He didn't like the name at first. But he's come around to it now. But I've been assessed by the early intervention team more times than I could count, and they always say I've got too much insight. So, I've never been under them. But last time they assessed me, they sent me all this paperwork, and in the paperwork was some advice. And one of the things was to give your hallucination a name, to make it more separate from you and remind you that it's separate. So, I gave him the name Nigel. If I was having a bad day, I'd go, 'Nigel bad today' and stuff like that. Now he does also respond to the name, but at first he didn't. He's taken about two years. Now if I go, 'Shut up, Nigel', sometimes he listens.

Michelle explained how she started hearing voices at an early age.

I would say, just growing up, I had this voice in my head, but I didn't know that not everyone had this voice in their head. And every time I would do anything, I hear this voice say, 'That was so stupid. That was so dumb. Why did you say that? That was wrong.' It's questioning me on everything that I did. And then at night, I would hear the voice in my head saying, 'Everything you did was so dumb today. You're a horrible, horrible person. I can't believe you said this, you did that. You're just an idiot.' And I would just be so devastated. So, it was paranoia, but it was something criticizing me all the time. And I thought if I would just be the right person, I wouldn't have this thought all the time. Because I didn't realize that not everybody had this. I thought I was just being so dumb all the time. And I didn't realize that I was being told that I was dumb from a voice of paranoia. I wasn't living my life.

THE GREMLINS AND THE CHAOS GREMLIN

I hear a range of voices. I live with bipolar disorder, and my hallucinations are linked to my moods. When I'm severely depressed, the voices are cruel, scary, and challenging to live with. When I'm manic (a mood state which involves an elevated mood, impulsiveness, and risk-taking behaviour), I hear a single voice which is motivating and affirms my ideas and goads me into impulsive actions.

The Chaos Gremlin' arrived first. The Gremlins came later. I first heard Chaos Gremlin as a teenager, but it wasn't until my first term at university that its impact on my life began to ramp up. It's strange to say, but it felt like a friend, a best friend who's always positive, always encouraging you, giving you ideas and filling you with confidence. It was a frequent visitor for most of my 20s and I often wished for it to turn up when I was stable and well. I hear it much less often now. Like how you see distant relatives every other year, or an old friend. I've had to wave goodbye to Chaos Gremlin many times, as its words and ideas became all-consuming and would cause my behaviour to become unpredictable. It would tell me to write down ideas and stories, which I would later look back at and see a scrawl of gibberish on the page. It would tell me the formula for time travel, which pretty much involved barrel rolling down a specific hill at a specific date and time. It was incredibly convincing. This would mean bipolar mania was in full swing, and I would be very unwell. Life was never boring with Chaos Gremlin and still, even now, I miss it.

The Gremlins are another story. I can't wait for them to leave so I can slam the door behind them. They usually appear when I'm feeling at my lowest, and they grab all the worst thoughts, words, and memories which pop into my head, to use against me. The Gremlins often sound like a group of people chatting, or whispering, or raucously laughing and shouting over one another. It can make day-to-day life difficult, as when I'm out and about during the day, or meeting up with friends for a night out, I find myself second-guessing if what I'm hearing is real or a hallucination. Sometimes their talk is impossible to decipher; other times it's crystal clear. When I do understand the Gremlins, it's a distressing and deeply upsetting experience. These Gremlins are linked to my low moods, but I've also heard them when I've been under extreme stress or had a particularly intense bout of insomnia.

From my own experience, I've shown how sometimes hallucinations can be a positive experience. This has been the case for both Chris and Sara.

Sara has had both negative and comforting hallucinations.

I'd say with auditory hallucinations. I think something a lot of people miss about it is often when you say you're hearing voices, it's a distressing experience, which for a lot of my experience has been that. It can be very negative and deplete your self-worth. But I've also had positive auditory voices that make me feel good about life and that I don't find distressing, and I actually find quite comforting sometimes. I think when you talk about that, a lot of people are like, 'But that doesn't make sense. You're hearing things that aren't real', but I think it's something that maybe people don't consider that it's not always a horrible, distressing experience.

Chris explains how he no longer finds hallucinations a distressing experience.

I don't get freaked out by them. I'm a curious person. So sometimes I'll be lying in bed. And the ceiling is warped and wriggling, and I'm not taking any drugs. I don't smoke weed. So, everything I see, it feels like I'm already stoned or something, just on life. But stuff used to freak me out like that, but it doesn't any more. And some of the hallucinations are comforting, and helped me, like if I have to go do groceries. Sometimes I'll get a 'Bertram' being like, 'Hey, this is your life here.' And if it's 'Chester', it's 'Hey, you might meet someone cool there', and I'm just walking. And it's so funny, because I've thought about it. When I'm walking in public, I must look normal, but what's happening in my head is completely neurodivergent.

Hallucinations, as with delusions, are on a spectrum of experience, and that's something missing from much of people's knowledge about psychosis. For this book, I dug out some of my old journals. I can't keep a daily journal to save my life, but something I did do a few years back was journal my auditory hallucinations. I felt, at the time, it could give me power and control over the sounds and voices I was hearing. Here's one of the entries from that time.

I think I've found the worst combination ever of physical and mental illness. Migraine, room spinning, and doubting my sanity as I hear voices while sat in bed. I'm feeling very vulnerable and scared. I've felt physically ill all day today. We went out for a meal with friends but had to cut it short because I thought I was going to pass out or fall over from being so dizzy. This week has been an emotional rollercoaster with my moods all over the place. I've been ecstatically happy and hyperactive, busy working away on new projects. In a startling contrast, I've felt hopeless, useless and deeply lost.

Now I'm home and sat in bed. The noises have started. I can

hear creaking. It sounds like it's coming from the bed, but I'm not moving. It won't stop. I've turned on my laptop and found the easiest but most distracting programme I can find, *Always Sunny*. It reminds me of hanging out on a cosy Friday night with my partner Jimi. A time when I was happy and not hallucinating. If I can focus on this, maybe the voices will leave me alone.

It isn't working. Now the creaking has turned into banging on the bedroom window. The banging is urgent, fast, and incredibly loud as if a fist is pounding on the window. The blinds are closed and I'm paranoid now that the banging is real, and someone is playing a joke on me. Should I get up and check? I really should. I've been to open the blinds and there was nothing there. It's windy outside, and all I could see were the bushes and trees swaying. The unpredictable and forcible wind today is mirroring my state of mind. The banging is making me really uncomfortable. I'll turn the volume up on the laptop to try and drown out the noise. It's not working. Fuck. What is my mind trying to tell me? How can I rationalize this or tell it to stop?

It's suddenly stopped, thank fuck for that. I can breathe again. The cat has leapt up on the bed and has curled up next to me. It's like she knows something is wrong. Stroking her and listening to her gentle purr is calming me down. I've just realized it's getting dark outside and I'm sitting in the bedroom with no lights on. But I don't want to get up because right now, sitting here, I'm not hearing anything scary or confusing. I don't want to jinx it.

Now it's dark and I'm still sitting in the bedroom, still too afraid to get up and turn the lights on. I can hear footsteps coming into the room; it must be my husband. I hear the bed creak as he sits down on it next to me. He says to me, 'Do you want any carrots? I think we need some more carrots for next week.' I'm confused. Why is he talking about carrots? I respond, 'Yeah, OK, I'll put carrots on the shopping list next week.' I hear him get up and walk out the room. I'm not sure if that conversation was real. It was weird and random, and now I feel really muddled and confused. I've turned the light on now so I could write this down.

Oh yay, here comes the shouting! I close my eyes and try and focus my mind. All I can hear is 'Fuck! Fuck!' 'Get the fuck out!' Can't take this anymore. I'm getting up. I realize I'm trembling, and I feel as if I've been shaken roughly by someone much stronger than me. I sit down next to my husband on the sofa. I ask him, 'Did you come in the bedroom earlier?' He replies, 'No, I've been in here the whole time. Why?' I can't be bothered to explain what's been happening. I'm still feeling overwhelmed by voices. I'm asking him about his game. He's playing *Elite Dangerous*. I love how enthusiastic he is about this game and the idea of space travel. I make myself listen to him intently, and the shouting starts to fade.

The problem with hearing voices is the paranoia afterwards. Is that banging from outside or in my head? Is that whispering in the background of the TV show I'm watching or in my mind? Unknown noises set my teeth on edge. I'm jumpy, full of panic with the fear it will start again.

At least I'm talking about it.

In Part III, I'll be describing the coping techniques I've put together over the years and sharing what works for our interviewees too.

Visual hallucinations

This is when you see something that isn't actually there.

- You may see objects that don't exist.
- You may see people who you may know or complete strangers who aren't actually there.
- You may see visual patterns, optical illusions, or lights.

Kody described to me how his visual hallucinations have changed since he has been on medication for schizophrenia.

So, my hallucinations now that I'm medicated are fairly similar to any one I would experience in my everyday life. So, they're never super drawn-out. They're never super unique in any way. It would just be like talking to a very dull person. And so I find myself constantly questioning if I'm talking to someone who isn't there, because they look like anyone else in my everyday life. And I find myself constantly having to find coping mechanisms to identify if the person I'm talking to is really there or not. Before I was medicated, I did experience different types of visual hallucinations – hallucinations where I would see faceless people were really common for me to see before medication. And then auditory hallucinations vary anywhere from one voice up to, like, if I'm really overwhelmed or really having bad symptoms, it can seem like a dozen different voices speaking at once – like I'm in a crowded diner, I hear a lot of people, or in a crowded café. That's the best way I can describe it. Sometimes it seems like none of them are even talking to me, just talking to each other. Just talking to talk.

I don't get reoccurring hallucinations. So, all of my hallucinations seem to be people that I don't recognize. And it's to the point where that's what makes it challenging for me to decipher if who I'm talking to is really there or not. I've never built enough of a relationship to be able to give a hallucination a name or anything like that. Auditory hallucinations, I definitely have some I hear that are voices I definitely have heard in the past, but I'm stable enough on medication where I don't talk back to auditory hallucinations, if I can help it. And even if I do, it's the same thing where I've never been able to establish a name or identity for any of them.

I suggested to Kody that it must be strange that his hallucinations look like mundane, regular people.

Yeah, that's what makes it challenging for me. And it's different from pre-meds, because pre-meds I would, like I said, hallucinate faceless people, things that were a little bit more terrifying, but made less sense in my everyday life, whereas it's really difficult to decipher a hallucination who looks exactly like a person in my everyday life.

Chris experiences visual and auditory hallucinations. He's found his own unique way to deal with the hallucinations, which regularly take the form of two distinct faces.

Honestly, it's just the faces always. I draw the faces because they're an abstract eye that's looking at me that I see sometimes and feel around me. And so they're the mean hallucinations that I sometimes I trust and sometimes I don't. And I can't tell because I'm a spiritual person, too. So, how I see these faces are they're basically helping me along day by day because they're pretty neutral as a hallucination. But I also deal with an amalgamation of another hallucination, which is Chester. And that's the energy of the smiling faces that look like they're creepy. But I honestly honour the faces the same way that I would honour the sun or the moon. I'm very, very much that kind of a person.

I'm very spiritual. But the hallucinations that are always there are the faces.

As people do with voices in auditory hallucinations, Chris has named the two faces he sees, Chester and Bertram.

Just as the smiling one that is just like, 'Hey!' and I hear that and it's so weird to explain. It's like a 'Looney Tunes cartoon running backwards' kind of energy, Chester can be very 'arghhh!' and I feel that within my veins and in my nervous system. But I think that's just, you could call it me, you can call it something else. But from my experience, that's how it came to me was, 'Oh, this thing that talks to you all the time is a Chester' and the other thing, Bertram, is like the devil on my shoulder, if that makes sense. It's important to be in touch with your darkness, but never unbalance it.

Olfactory hallucinations

This one is to do with your sense of smell. You might begin to smell something strange and unpleasant which you can't place or figure out where it's coming from. It can also include scents and smells you like.

Libby explained to me how she previously experienced olfactory hallucinations.

So, I used to get olfactory hallucinations. I don't any more. But I used to smell blood a lot, the very strong iron smell. And it was the very distinctive smell of blood. I don't know why I keep saying 'I don't know why' as if there is a reason! I think that's something that's really annoying about me, though, is I'm always trying to find logical answers for things. And when it comes to psychosis, often there is no logical answer!

Tactile hallucinations

Tactile is to do with touch or feeling movement in or on your body. You could feel as though there are bugs or snakes crawling on your skin – this type of tactile hallucination is called formication. You might feel your skin is stretched over your head or feel someone's hands are touching you. It can feel as if your internal organs are moving or your skin is itching or burning.

Libby described to me her infrequent experience of tactile hallucinations.

I feel like it's very stereotypical, but bugs crawling on me. I don't really know where it's come from. I feel sometimes they just pop up out of nowhere. And I've been feeling that a lot. And then I get ones where it's almost like my skin is burning. How you imagine a piece of paper burning and it shrivels up and almost like my skin is doing that. It doesn't really hurt. But I can feel the sensations of it wrinkling; they're just strange. They used to really scare me at first, and sometimes the one with bugs still makes me panic. And because I'm constantly looking like, 'Are there bugs on me?' and then I'm constantly scratching my skin. And sometimes I end up taking the skin off from it, so that's not good. Now they're more frustrating than anything.

Gustatory hallucinations

These affect your sense of taste. You may have a strange or unpleasant taste in your mouth, or food you normally enjoy tastes 'off'. It often involves a metallic taste in your mouth.

Kinaesthetic hallucinations

This is when it feels as if your body is moving in an unusual way, when you're standing, lying down, sitting still, or even walking. It usually manifests as feeling as though you're flying or floating.

In Part III, we'll be taking a closer look at how to take care of yourself and live well, where I'll be sharing, alongside all the interviewees, tried and tested ways to keep yourself well and plan for when things get tough. We'll also look at what to do if you're hoping to support someone who experiences any of these hallucinations or delusions.

PART II
STIGMA AND PSYCHOSIS

I n Part II, I'll be taking a closer look at stigma and discrimination, and how it affects people with psychosis. Stigma can
be cripplingly difficult to deal with and affects all aspects of
modern life. As we have seen with myth-busting so far, stigma is
real, and in Part II we'll be looking in detail where stigma crops
up in our daily lives. I'll be breaking stigma down into short
chapters ranging from work, education, and daily life, family
and friends, race and ethnicity, social media, medical and mental health professionals, prison services, media, and pop culture.
I'll also be talking about why stigma against psychosis is still
so prevalent, the history of psychosis, and your rights if you're
discriminated against. It's not all doom and gloom, as I'll be
focusing too on how we combat stigma, how we can navigate
difficult conversations, and how we can inform, educate, and
spread awareness.

I'll also be taking a look at language. When someone misuses
the words 'psychosis', 'psychotic', or 'psycho', people immediately
jump to their preconceived notion of the illness. They see what

their experience of it is, what they have heard and seen in the media. It causes us to stereotype without really realizing that's what we're doing. When someone says to me, 'That's psychotic', it makes me feel that this diagnosis defines me – that my personality and the essence of what makes me who I am has dwindled down to a mental illness. All that I am is psychotic, and this is all anyone ever sees. It impacts my self-esteem in a significant way. It is limiting and dehumanizing. It takes away our individuality to be spoken about in this way. Although I believe labels are important and a tool to receive treatment and provide answers to behaviours, being seen as just a label can be damaging.

There is still a huge issue with how we use language to explain mental illness. With mental illnesses, you're seen as weak. You're not seen as blameless. When you have a psychotic break, nobody ever tells you, 'Well, it's just one of those things.' Instead, you're seen as a failure and told, 'You could be doing more to help yourself.' Psychosis isn't a weakness or failure on our part, but the misuse of language continues to contribute to the stigma.

It's important that we use language delicately and with care when discussing psychosis. Think about how much impact your words have and how they can shape a person's self-worth. I'll be exploring how we can use language sensitively and how to explain to somebody when you find their use of language difficult or offensive.

When I originally pitched this book, the subject of stigma was going to fit into one chapter. As I started to structure the book and sat down and thought about what needed to be said, I realized stigma was a far bigger topic and I had to devote a much bigger chunk of my word count to it – it simply couldn't be contained in a single chapter! This book is all about myth-busting, and you can't pop the bubble of an idea without first understanding stigma and where it comes from.

Chapter 5
What Are Stigma and Discrimination?

In Part II, we're looking at stigma and discrimination. First off, let's briefly look at those words and what they mean:

> Stigma is a negative attitude, prejudice, or false belief. It's often a societal belief, a widely held attitude in society, or a prejudice held by a group of people.

Stigma causes a group of people (in this instance, people with psychosis) to feel devalued and believe others think less of them, look down on them, or are less worthy of support and love than other people. Someone who holds stigmatizing views may decide to discriminate against, in this situation, people with psychosis.

> Discrimination is when you are treated differently in a workplace, educational setting, or in your community because of stigma.

Discrimination boils down to being treated unfairly because of psychosis you experience or have experienced. Discrimination manifests in varying ways.

You could be discriminated against directly, such as being turned down for a tenancy or being evicted.

It might be indirect – for example, when there's a policy or rule which has a negative effect on you because you have psychosis, such as receiving a disciplinary warning for having time off work because of a psychotic episode.

You may experience harassment – behaviour that is unwanted, offensive, and distressing. Someone might try to make you feel intimidated or humiliated through their words or actions.

You might ask for reasonable adjustments to be made at your job to help you work, but a manager refuses to make those changes.

Awareness fatigue

I've seen a shift recently in how people view advocacy and stigma around mental illness. To some, it's now 'boring' – the heavy lifting has already been done and raising awareness is no longer necessary or needed. I think they're wrong.

To say we are at a saturation point of awareness coverage, or we need to move on, I think underestimates the stigma many individuals with psychosis and related disorders still face. It's almost naive and I think sometimes comes from a position of privilege. Some mental illnesses are talked about more than others. They're more accessible and easier to digest and for people to relate to. Certain groups are more willing to listen, accept, and support someone with a mental illness. When you mix in other prejudices which people cope with (racism, homophobia, transphobia, for instance) which exacerbate mental ill health, these issues need to be addressed.

It worries me that with this attitude, there will instead be a shift in focus in the media, to another cause or issue that feels more relevant or needs addressing. Our valid concerns about psychosis stigma won't be discussed. Changing public perceptions of psychosis shows the public how serious this is and why it's so important that we can all access quality, prompt care to mental health services when we need it. Awareness educates and informs and sways public opinion to standing up for our cause. We often talk about reducing stigma/raising awareness or the need for more funding for mental health services, but why are they seen as mutually exclusive? Surely, we can talk about both issues and still help to create change. This conversation, as so many have labelled it, is far-reaching and means different things to different people.

The problem with the term 'mental health'

'We all have mental health!' Which is true, and I have no problem with people discussing their individual experiences. My problem is that vital voices are being drowned out. 'Mental health' has become this huge umbrella of different meanings. The ideas that are more accessible and easier to digest for the general public will undoubtedly receive more attention.

It feels mental health is becoming increasingly synonymous with wellbeing, mindfulness, and self-care. Again, all great if you struggle occasionally with the stresses of life or have a mild mental illness. They're not for everyone and they certainly aren't a magic cure. I'm growing more and more concerned that these subjects will shift the idea of what mental illness is and trivialize it. I don't need to read any more articles about mindfulness – I get it, I know what it's about. I don't want people to start preaching to me about how if I practised self-care and had a hot bubble bath with some aromatherapy candles, I could break out of a psychotic episode. No, what would do that is a review of my medication and the support of my psychiatrist.

It's all got confused and muddled. I mean, there have been many fantastic, impactful anti-stigma campaigns, but I think, in some ways, they've confused people. It's important we all listen when someone with psychosis wants to take the floor.

We need people who talk about bipolar disorder, psychosis, and schizophrenia – voices that have the right platform and are listened to, because these aren't easy subjects to open up about. It feels terrifying to begin with: the real fear of being judged and ridiculed, stigmatized for something you have truly little control over. By using the term 'mental health', these important discussions are being lumped in with articles about adult colouring books and how to meditate. Self-help articles, in my opinion, should not be compared with articles educating about severe mental illness. There is a vast difference between the two.

As an example, I recently had a conversation with someone about my writing. and I mentioned that I often write about mental health. She instantly started talking to me about how she's sometimes anxious while flying and how she's managed it through thinking positively. That's great and I was genuinely pleased for her. When I started talking about what I write about and how I regularly write about psychosis, I could see her eyes widen. She quickly changed the subject. This is the problem. Anything beyond being anxious on a plane was too much for her to handle. I used the term 'mental health', and I gave her a response she wasn't expecting. If I'd said I wrote about mental *illness*, I think her expectations would have been different.

We need conversations about how those with severe mental illness are not all dangerous but are more likely to be the victims of violence and crime. We need conversations about how poverty, housing, and being an ethnic minority or part of the LGBTQ+ community can have a negative impact on mental health.

Maybe it's time for a new term or a shift in how people use the terms we already have. If you're writing about general wellbeing, say that. If you're writing about mental illness, then say that too. Don't jumble up the two – it's causing more harm than good.

For many people, as soon as the term 'mental health' is brought up, what comes to mind is depression and anxiety. In no way am I trying to say that depression and anxiety aren't important – they can be crippling and severe. The problem here is that so much emphasis is put on these conditions, but we must speak up about all mental illnesses.

The general public can relate to depression and anxiety as they're more common. Chances are, they themselves – or someone they're close to – have suffered from these conditions. It's easy to forget about psychosis when you have no real-life experience of it.

When I've brought up the subject of mental illness and my struggles with psychosis with people, their first response is usually along the lines of, after a long pause, 'I get anxious/depressed sometimes.'

It's great that they can feel honest and open with me, but that wasn't the point of the conversation. People will often turn a conversation around into something they can relate to. Talking about psychosis makes people uncomfortable and often they don't know how to respond.

These conditions that are less talked about are also more stigmatized. With psychosis, you're seen as crazy, as though you could snap and murder someone at any moment. Continuing to not pay psychosis any attention leaves sufferers feeling incredibly isolated and alone.

We need to raise awareness of all conditions under the mental illness umbrella. Ignoring conditions because the conversation is harder to start will only further alienate sufferers. Allow people to share their story. Their experiences are valid and important.

Romanticizing psychosis

Psychosis should never be an aspiration. There's one phrase which makes my blood boil: 'cute but psycho'.

Making it seem cute, romantic, or beautiful distorts what it's actually like to experience. This way of thinking cultivates the idea that something like psychosis is romantic. That it's a quirk, something that makes you special and unique. This viewpoint completely devalues the struggle of people who experience psychosis. How are we meant to be taken seriously when people continue to romanticize it or see it as a personality quirk? All this does is undo the work of others trying to educate.

There's still a long way to go in educating about psychosis. People are quick to judge and repeat stigmatizing myths they've heard. Not everyone is confident enough to call people out. It still makes my heart race when I do. This compounds the problem when people's views go unchallenged. If you can point people in the right direction, it can make an enormous difference.

People seem to hold on to the idea that psychosis can make you more interesting. Being 'cute but psycho' will make you sound edgy and vibrant, and the type of person people want to be around. The crux of it is this: saying psychosis is a cute, quirky trait tells people who have a negative, brutal, and unrelentingly bad experience that if only they tried harder, then they could see it your way too. But it doesn't work that way. How about praising people for getting through a psychotic episode? How about listening and being a good, supportive friend? How about actively being part of the change in perceptions of psychosis? These are things we should all aspire to.

History of psychosis

Many people believe psychosis is a modern illness, but in reality only the word 'psychosis' is relatively new. People across the globe have experienced hallucinations and delusions for millennia. The term 'psychosis' was first coined in 1845, but written evidence goes back as far as 3000 years ago. The next time someone says:

'Psychosis is a new thing!'

'People didn't used to have psychosis, they just got on with life!'

'Psychosis is just made up'

tell them how far back accounts of delusions and hallucinations go. Let's take a closer look at some examples.

Descriptions of psychosis go back to the beginning of the written history of China, dating back to the Shang Dynasty, 3000 years ago. Psychosis with or without epilepsy was described as an 'imbalance', and [visual illusions] were also described as a separate illness (Bürgy 2008).

In the ancient civilization of Babylon (626–539 BC), cuneiform tablets describe delusions of persecution and extreme paranoia. It was called *Maqlu*, translated as 'the burning'. To release the persecutors from a patient's mind, a priest/doctor would burn or melt images of wood or wax in front of them (Reynolds *et al.* 2014).

Writings in Indian medicine describe symptoms of psychosis as early as the fifth century BC.

Also in the fifth century BC, in ancient Greece, Herodotus wrote his *Histories* which depicted hallucinations.

When many people think of the history of psychosis, they think of medieval Europe, demonic possession, and witch burning. It's one of the reasons psychosis is still so stigmatized. As you can see from the above, long before witch trials and exorcisms, humans were trying to understand and treat psychosis in a logical and compassionate way.

Race and ethnicity

When we talk about stigma, it's important to factor in race and ethnicity. It's vital to recognize privilege if you have it, and the inequalities in mental health care, treatment by police, and the way a psychotic episode is viewed depending on your race and ethnicity.

As a white person, I felt it was important to share voices from other communities. Even though I'm from a working-class background, I do have privilege, and my experiences of psychosis and the treatment I've received will differ from someone from an ethnic minority background.

Chris told me about how being part of an Indigenous community shaped his view of psychosis.

I grew up in an environment that was spiritual, but it was like spirituality from within you. Instead of looking out in the world for a sign, it's more focused on respect to each other, chill, wait for ideas to come, create some. And that's how it's been with my culture. We're called the Mi'gmaw people. I'm white skin as hell because my dad is Scottish. But I grew up in the Indigenous setting, and voices and hallucinations and things like that were never a problem. It was only a problem if it started getting twisted. They don't instantly jump on you for hearing voices and try to get you somewhere. They just go, 'Oh, OK.' I guess from the Indigenous perspective, I grew up on a reserve, multiple people hear voices, and people have a lot of experiences that are spiritual. I've learned over time that spirituality isn't all the trinkets. I call it the trinkets because it's like the distracting shiny stuff that makes people go toward it. But for me, spirituality is I put my hand on my knee and then a dragonfly lands on my hand. That's beautiful. That's magical.

My grandfather told me before he died, that there's no word in Mi'gmaw for schizophrenia. And I asked him why. And he said, 'Because it's the test of the spirits. We don't have a word for it. It's just a test of spirits.' And that changed my whole perspective on how to take care of myself. To connect back in the world. He said the right thing at the right time. And he wasn't even trying to be like, he was just casual. Like, 'Yeah, the test of the spirits, Chris.' And I'm like, 'What!?' Rest in peace, you magnificent, man.

I also spoke to Earl Pennycooke from the USEMI Racial Trauma Clinic and the Psychosis Therapy Project about how psychosis stigma affects ethnic minority groups:

Black men are more likely to experience psychosis and a misdiagnosis of this term. Often people who are re-experiencing trauma are seen as psychotic. Ethnic minority group clients with autism may also be misdiagnosed with psychosis. An individual has to deal with the diagnosis or misdiagnosis and their family may feel ashamed that one of their family members suffers from this mental health issue. Any diagnosis is a lifetime diagnosis without the recognition that some people recover after being in hospital.

It has a knock on effect in the community, which by large are mistrusting of psychiatric services. They see a continual decline in their loved one's psychological wellbeing as there is little or no help in the community. The latest figures show that Black women are more likely to experience common mental health issues such as anxiety or depression more than their white counterparts. Older South Asian women are at risk of suicide. The recovery rates for ethnic minority groups are far lower than their white counterparts.

Professionals, mental health services, and race and ethnicity

I asked Earl Pennycooke from the USEMI Racial Trauma Clinic and the Psychosis Therapy Project about how to improve the relationship between professionals, mental health services, and ethnic minority groups:

> I feel that we have to decolonise the thinking of psychiatric professionals both white and non white practitioners. This can be done where regular meetings can take place between professionals and the local community, to break down any misunderstandings they may have of each other. Also, I believe that the professionals have to listen to what the individual or the community are saying rather than the professionals imposing their will on the individual through the lens that they are the experts. It's clear that from the outside that you have to look at what are the major cultural factors and influences in the individual's life. By this I mean you take into account someone's race, class, religion or lack of religion and sexual identity and background to have a better understanding of what the individual is experiencing at that time.

Also for the practitioners to work closer to family and friends in the community to provide a more trauma informed approach and response.

Earl also shared how services can change to serve ethnic minority groups better:

I think any cultural barriers that are not recognized have to be addressed. One of the big factors not being thought about is how trauma is affecting the individual and how they're maybe experiencing generational trauma coupled with being from an immigrant family and at times living in poverty. I feel that it's important that the service is representative of the community that it works in, such as by having a diverse workforce and delivering culturally appropriate services. Through the work with communities, they should aim to break down stereotypes and unconscious biases and having equality and diversity at the heart of the work in the communities that they work in.

Chapter 6

Why Is There Still So Much Stigma Surrounding Psychosis?

I asked each interviewee this question, and the results were pretty unanimous:

'People don't understand what psychosis is.'

It's the first hurdle, and still many people aren't even making an attempt to jump over. They're walking over to it, inspecting the hurdle, deciding it's too high, too risky a leap to take. They're turning round back to where they started with a massive 'NOPE!'

What people don't often realize is this:

'Stigma can be just as damaging as psychosis itself.'

So, it's vital that we devote time to talking about it and why it exists. Jen told me how before her own psychotic episode, she had very little knowledge of psychosis or what it meant to experience it.

I think because there's a lack of understanding. Before I was psychotic, I didn't even know what psychosis was. I wouldn't know what it was; I would just associate it with someone being mad and completely off their rocker. But I think there's a lack of understanding, and that leads to fear, and people are afraid of things they don't know. So, because of the fear, it leads to stigma – because they're afraid of what they don't know about psychosis. That just leads to a lack of understanding and a fear and a stigma.

It doesn't matter what your background is, or your education level, or your job, psychosis can happen to anyone.

From my own experience, it wasn't until I started putting the pieces together of the psychotic symptoms I'd had in the past that I started to research what psychosis was. It led me to realize I'd been experiencing psychosis, which was later confirmed by a psychiatrist. If I hadn't looked up 'hearing voices' on Google, it probably would've taken a serious psychotic episode and hospitalization for me to know what was happening.

But this wasn't idle curiosity: I knew something was wrong. And let's be honest, how many times have you randomly looked up the word 'psychosis', 'psychotic', or 'delusional' because you wanted to learn more? I'm guessing probably never. That's why it's so important to talk to people about psychosis if you're able to. People aren't looking for the information, and sometimes it's because they already believe they know the answer.

As a teenager, I was guilty of misunderstanding what psychosis was. Like a typical overconfident, self-assured teenager, I thought I knew better than everyone, and this included my knowledge of psychosis, which was categorically wrong. That knowledge came from TV and the media.

Kody explains how the portrayal of people with psychosis in the media is skewed towards the negative.

I think it's because of how it's portrayed in the media, still; they tend to not draw any attention to mental illness unless it's negative. I feel there are plenty of people living very comfortably with mental illness. And so, when they only show the negative sides of that, I think it can really make it hard for people to see that people with mental illness, specifically with psychosis-related disorders…if they only ever see that they're really negative, then that's going to be how they view it, because they're not going to know any other portrayal of it.

If we're only ever fed negative views on *any* subject, it will slant our opinion and make us less open and receptive to learning more. If you're told 'this thing always looks like this' or 'people with this issue will always act this way', why would you go out of your way to find new information?

Psychosis is seen as a taboo subject. It shouldn't be, but one of the reasons is not just a lack of understanding but also how people who don't experience it struggle to relate. You can explain what hallucinations and delusions are to someone, give them examples, and even share your experiences, but sometimes people just don't get it.

Hazel told me about how they believe psychosis is sometimes just too far removed from people's own life experience.

I think part of it is it's harder to understand. So yes, people might not fully understand what depression or anxiety are, but they at least know what the terms mean. They have an idea of what it feels like to be depressed, in that they've felt sad before. Even though I know that depression is actually much more complicated than that. They've got an idea of what it is to have an anxiety disorder because they've probably felt anxious at some point, stressed at some point – they've got a point of reference. Unless someone's taken drugs, or not slept for four days, they've probably never experienced anything even similar to psychosis. Therefore, it's something so outside of their experiences that they end up making us into an outgroup or 'othering' us, which, psychologically speaking, makes perfect sense, because it's what we used to do when we were in tribes – but in the modern day, not so useful, not so helpful. I think also by 'othering' people, they're making it almost like our failing, and therefore saving themselves in their mind from it. I think that's what it is. I think it's partly self-preservation. They're othering us to keep themselves safe, because it means that they're not at risk.

There are advocates out there talking about psychosis. However, many mainstream mental health advocates discuss psychosis, without ever experiencing it themselves. This can be dangerous and damaging, as their followers will believe their viewpoint and trust their opinion, even if there are inaccuracies. As they are mental health advocates, and because they've been through a mental illness, people will trust what they're saying is right. The reality is, if you haven't experienced psychosis, you're going to get a lot of it wrong. Unknowingly adding to the stigma is just as harmful, but it can also go unchallenged, and the mistake is never publicly rectified.

What has happened with mental health advocates is that a few names become synonymous with 'mental health' in the media. The same faces are seen talking about a variety of topics surrounding mental illness. What happens when an advocate with psychosis wants to start talking about it? They're pushed aside or never considered, because those big-name advocates have already cemented their place.

A massive obstacle when we're trying to create understanding of psychosis is when the person listening is secretly thinking, 'It will never happen to me!'

Libby told me how many people feel they will never experience psychosis because they don't have a certain lifestyle.

I think people with psychosis are too afraid to talk about it. And people without it are too scared to talk about it, but for different reasons. People without psychosis, I think either they don't understand it and so they think it's something really scary. They think, 'Part of me wants to use the word "disgusting"', and they turn their noses up at it, and they think, 'Oh, that only happens to this group of people.' Or, because a lot of psychosis is a result of substance abuse, people think they're above that kind of thing. And so, when you put those two together, people don't talk about it because they think it's beneath them. I think that happens a lot.

When we look down at a group of people, we're not taking the time to fully understand them and why they got to where they are. Anyone can experience psychosis. Yes, it sometimes has a link to drug use, but, again, how did someone get there? The same goes for our mental health. None of us are invulnerable to developing a mental illness at some point. Most of us are a few missed pay cheques away from losing a home, or not being able to afford the rent. We're all vulnerable to the same things; some of us are lucky, some of us aren't.

Psychosis is not just one experience. As shown in Part I, hallucinations and delusions are a huge array of experiences which greatly vary from person to person. Everyone experiences psychosis differently, even when they have the same symptoms. With so many inaccurate depictions on our television screens and at the movies, which mostly centre around violence, horror, and fear, this point is not obvious to many people.

Sara explains how people are often not aware that psychosis is on a spectrum.

I think it's just so misunderstood. One of the main reasons for that is television and film and things like that do not help. They always home in on stereotypes. They always choose the most violent people. They'll say, 'Oh, this person's murdered this many people, and they happen to have this diagnosis.' And a lot of people tune in on that and think, 'Oh, well, that must mean what it is.' But I think that people don't understand what psychosis actually entails and how it can manifest. There's so many different experiences; it's not just a one-size-fits-all. It's a very wide spectrum. And I think, there needs to be so much more education on it, because it is a lot more common than people think. It was always portrayed to me as this rare thing that very, very few people had. And as I've got older, I have just realized that so many people have experienced it, or are experiencing it, or have illnesses. I think that the lack of education and the lack of awareness about what it's like and what it can entail is a massive reason for that.

How do we help people understand psychosis?

How do you help someone see psychosis isn't a mysterious, alien, other worldly concept, but instead as just another part of the multifaceted human experience?

- **Use your myth-busting facts.** As a nerdy gamer who loves science fiction and could probably write a book on how *Deep Space Nine* is the best and most underrated

Star Trek series, I have many logical-thinking friends who love facts. Present facts to them, and they're ready to be beamed on board. This is where the facts from Part I come into play and can show someone what psychosis is and definitely isn't.

- **Show them media with positive representations of psychosis.** This doesn't have to be from a TV show or movie. It could be a documentary, podcast, a YouTube channel, a video game, or a book. Save positive and informative interviews that you may hear from media outlets on your phone or computer to share later. Or send links to friends – just ask them if they actually watched it! I've added some examples in the resources section at the end of the book.

- **Use social media for good.** Follow, share, and encourage others to follow accounts advocating for psychosis awareness. That means lived-experience accounts and mental health professionals, depending on what you want people in your life to have a clearer idea of. Examples of who to follow are in this book! Most of the interviewees are active on social media and regularly share their own stories and educate their followers on psychosis. Their social media handles are included at the end of the book.

- **Frame your experiences in a new way.** When you're explaining hallucinations and delusions, think about the person you're talking to. What life experiences do they have which you could use to broaden their understanding of psychosis? For example, my partner Jimi works with computers. I often frame ideas about psychosis around IT concepts, so we can have a shared frame of reference. For instance, I've compared my brain feeling full and busy when I'm hearing voices to a computer updating – it's slow to respond and takes longer or might not be able to do some tasks. Or when I've had a psychotic episode and I've needed to speak to a medical professional, I'll explain it as my brain needing a reboot.

How does stigma affect the lives and behaviour of people with psychosis?

Stigma against psychosis isn't just a nuisance, like a fly you can swat away and eventually it moves on. Stigma sticks around, like a gnat on a humid day. When you put together everything that contributes to stigma, it can feel like a massive weight to bear. Stigma negatively affects people with psychosis and how they live their daily lives. For many people with psychosis, it becomes about self-preservation. If they stay quiet, they won't have to deal with any fallout.

Libby, a psychology student, sums up how many people with psychosis feel.

> People with psychosis, they get really scared to talk about it because they don't want to be judged. And they don't want to be misunderstood. I think that happens quite a lot, and I think people, they just want to protect themselves. And a lot of the time the only way to do that is to not talk about it at all, or only talk about it in your inner circles. So, then no conversation is happening because neither side wants to talk about it. Which makes it really difficult to dismantle things like stigma.

Stigma also leads to internalized stigma. This is when someone with psychosis begins to believe the negative views people have of psychosis. Internalized stigma can be incredibly damaging and can lead to low self-esteem and and depression. It can also be a significant barrier for someone to seek out help and support.

It's important for people who have little to no experience of what psychosis is to understand how deeply stigma impacts people who live with it. It is a big deal and waving it away as inconsequential won't help anyone. Instead of looking at 'sides' or who's right and who's wrong, a conversation about stigma should start with:

'This is a person with a different perspective to mine. They have life experience I don't. Maybe I should listen to what they have to say. I might learn something new.'

People with psychosis have more to lose when they open up, or when they try to educate friends, family, and acquaintances. If you don't have psychosis, all you risk is a bit of awkwardness. That's it. That's the risk. It's OK to be wrong, and it's OK to not have all the facts. Humans are fallible; we make mistakes. What also makes us human is our ability to think critically, to analyse an issue, and to learn and internalize new ideas. Put ego aside and listen to someone with lived experience – they're the experts on their own circumstances.

In Part II, we're looking at all of these reasons and more, and how we as individuals, organizations, and charities can work together to try to eradicate this stigma.

Chapter 7

Stigma and Discrimination in Work and Daily Life

Life can be difficult to navigate when you have psychosis, especially when you're faced with stigma and discrimination. All eight interviewees for this book told me they'd experienced stigma in their daily life. Either from a partner, friends, family or in education and work. The majority also told me about discrimination they'd experienced for having psychosis.

Friends

Jen experienced stigma from friends after she had experienced psychosis, but with the added difficulty of having been arrested because of her actions while delusional.

> I think I have (experienced stigma) because of the criminal part of psychosis. I think that really wasn't understood by a lot of my friends. And they cut off my friendship because of that. So, I think I have experienced stigma from some of my actions during psychosis. Some of my threats I made were towards them,

so they cut off ties, because they didn't really understand why I made threats against them, which is understandable. But even when I apologized, they still didn't understand. A lot of them have forgiven me. Some of them just couldn't understand it.

I asked Jen how it felt when she was recovering, trying to explain her experience, but people weren't getting it.

It made me feel quite upset and sad about how my friends didn't understand that I was unwell at the time. And that normally, I would never say things like that. It was just me completely psychotic and deluded. And completely unwell. A lot of them didn't understand that. So, it took some time. Some people have come back to me saying they now understand it. So, it's not all doom and gloom. I found that in my case, people are willing to learn about it and hang around. But I find that particularly heart wrenching when you've been really unwell, and you explain it and they just go, no.

Partners

I'm lucky to be in a long-term relationship, with someone who is willing to listen and learn about psychosis. It wasn't always this way, and for others like me, relationships can end because of stigma. From partners using psychosis against you in arguments, calling you 'crazy', 'psycho', or 'psychotic' to hurt you in the heat of the moment, it does happen. They may witness unusual behaviour before you're ready to openly talk about it, and not know how to respond, and even be scared. It can be devastating to have a partner use something you have no control over against you, or simply not be willing or able to understand. It can make you feel broken, and make you question what kind of person you are. You may be left thinking, 'maybe they're right about me?'

Moving forward to when I first told Jimi, my long-term partner, that I had psychotic episodes, and I was terrified. It took me a week of building up the courage to talk to him and my nerves were fraught with worry. I remember he went noticeably quiet and my brain was shouting at me, 'THIS IS NOT A GOOD SIGN, ABORT! ABORT!' But people react differently to news, and with Jimi, silence meant he was processing what I'd told him. He told me he wanted to go away to think about what I'd said, and what he did was take learning into his own hands and research what psychosis was actually about. When we spoke again the next day, he told me what he'd learned and had come back with questions. I remember the lump in my throat and my eyes beginning to sting with tears. I couldn't have asked for a better response.

Family

Generational gaps can be difficult to navigate, especially if you're from a family which isn't emotionally open. Or a family where psychosis is the type of subject where the response you get is usually…

'We don't talk about that sort of thing.'

Crossing that divide is important, and how we frame conversations around psychosis might have to be different from how we speak to friends. Older family members might be afraid of saying the wrong thing, getting something wrong, and accidentally pushing you away, so they'd rather stay quiet and, from their point of view, keep the peace.

Chris told me how his family don't always understand psychosis, but their intentions always come from a place of love.

> When I was going through the worst of my psychosis, it was like they were too afraid to talk to me. And that hurt me in that state. Because even though I look freaky, I would never hurt anybody. I'm actually hoping someone gives me a hug. And so, when my family reacted adversely, it was like, 'Oh, you're crazy.' Then I felt like, 'Oh, stigma. Great.' Coming from my own family, which I least expected because they were all so supportive at the beginning. Stigma is also talking to someone and then when you mention you have bipolar or schizophrenia or whatever, they just go, 'OK, cool, nice.' And they walk away. Because I'll say like, 'Hey, I don't feel too well.' And their only frame of reference is a stomach ache, or a migraine. And I'm like, 'This is the kind of "I don't feel well" where it's affecting my reality. So please, can someone listen?' I've been missing my family a lot. We still talk to each other. But because I got delusional, and I was being kind of weird, they backed off for a bit, but they don't hate me. They love me. They're just confused because they don't know a lot about this stuff. But they keep comparing me to my grandpa. And that makes me happy. Because I love my grandpa. They're supportive again now, but I've had to deal with things like that in my life.

Work and volunteering

Not everyone who works and who has psychosis experiences stigma and discrimination, as in both the UK and the US you don't need to disclose a disability to your workplace, and this includes a mental illness.

Hazel describes how even when those in the workplace aren't aware, stigma can still be harmful.

I feel that if I was able to talk about things earlier, when the red flags were there, then maybe I wouldn't get into crisis. Also, you wouldn't feel stressed about people finding out. Whenever I do have a job, I get so stressed about people maybe finding out that I won't take sick days when I should. I'll work more hours than I should to try to prove that I'm productive. And I think I make myself ill in those situations, in part because I'm so obsessed, I'm overcompensating, I'm so paranoid about someone finding out I'm ill – and therefore me losing my job – that I make myself ill by overcompensating and then lose my job!

Kody explains how workplaces can be supportive, but also how he wished he had disclosed mental illness in previous jobs.

I've had difficulty holding jobs in the past. My more recent job I've had, they were very understanding about my symptoms, they allowed me to leave if I started having symptoms. I was very open and honest with my HR rep and the manager at the store. And they both were very understanding of my symptoms and let me go if I started having issues, and in the past, I didn't have as much luck with that. A lot of times, looking back now, I think maybe I could have been able to navigate workplaces a little bit better had I disclosed the information to someone in HR, to someone in the workplace, but I would usually not say anything because of the stigma surrounding the workplace. There are definitely times, at school, work, and the local community, I think there's been times in every one of these scenarios where I've experienced some sort of discrimination, but I also never disclosed it. So it was more that people didn't know what was going on with me. It was before I had a diagnosis, it was before I had gotten treatment. I went a few years, very delusional, and having a lot of hallucinations before I finally got any help. And so I definitely think, had I disclosed the illness and people still treated me the way I did, I would look at it as discrimination, but I think it more became that they didn't know how to help me because I wasn't even willing to help myself at the time.

Your rights and how to help others

Good workplaces won't discriminate and will make sure there are accommodations in place so that you feel supported to do your job. However, it can be tricky to judge just how a manager, an HR rep, or work colleague will react. Even though it's illegal in the US and UK to fire someone or refuse to hire them because of a mental illness, it still happens and can be difficult to prove.

Your rights will differ depending on where you live.

If you live in the UK, it's all about the Equality Act 2010, and in the US the one to remember is the Americans with Disabilities Act (ADA). Both were put in place to protect anyone with a disability. Disability also encompasses mental illness and therefore psychosis. Let's look more closely at these laws.

Equality Act 2010 protects you in the workplace. It includes if you're made redundant, fired, or applying for a job and you can prove these actions were taken due to discrimination. You can challenge informally through the company, or you can make a claim to an Employment Tribunal. You might be offered financial compensation if your claim is successful.

The Equality Act also means you don't have to disclose mental illness, and you can't be asked if you have a mental illness at an interview or in the workplace.

American with Disabilities Act (ADA) aims to makes sure

those with disabilities have the same rights and opportunities as anyone else. Employers are expected to make reasonable adjustments and accommodations for applicants and employees to be able to do their job.

You don't have to disclose a mental illness at interview. If you need to have a medical exam before starting a job, the job offer can't be withdrawn – unless you can't fulfil the role even with reasonable adjustments.

There isn't an easy solution, and the way society is set up means discrimination is rife in workplaces. Capitalist value systems are based around your productivity and what you can contribute to the economy, and that is why rules and laws like these have been introduced. But they're not foolproof.

What to do when someone in your life doesn't understand

When we see someone we care about who's struggling, is going through a tough time, or is unwell, our go-to gut reaction is *I need to fix this*. When it comes to psychosis, partners, friends, and family often don't understand and because psychosis seems to them this mysterious monolith they can't decode – they don't know how to fix it. The fear factor amps up – fear of not knowing, fear of what this means for your relationship, fear of a distance between you and them. And then, 'How do I even talk to this person?' People often see psychosis as a taboo subject, or the kind of conversation where 'it's never the right time'.

From my own experience, I've seen panic in the eyes of people I care about, terrified they'll put their foot in it, say the wrong thing, alienate me, or push me over the metaphorical edge of sanity. So instead of talking to me, asking questions, or offering support, they clam up and stay silent. It's easy to see from their point of view that they believe they're doing the right thing.

Communication, though, actively listening to the other person and not being a bystander in a conversation, is far more impactful.

What can we do?

There are a few points we can make to drive home how important communication is.

- Explain that they can't fix psychosis and that's OK.
- Explain what works is to help make living with psychosis a little easier and life a little better, and sharing what that looks like for you.
- Silence is worse than getting it wrong. It's better to have a conversation about what works and what doesn't than to stay silent.
- Trying and failing to understand psychosis is better than never bothering at all.

When you talk to someone, make it personal. What I mean by that is telling them how it makes you feel, rather than about what they're getting wrong. You could say:

- When you ask, 'How can I help?' it makes me feel supported and loved.
- When you ask questions about psychosis, it makes me feel as if I'm valued and worth it.
- When you say something that isn't helpful, it's OK because I know you care enough to try.
- When you try to understand how psychosis affects me, it makes me feel heard, understood, and cared for.

It's all about willingness to learn. A friend or family member might never completely understand, but wanting to is just as important.

Listening is important here too. They might want to learn, but they also need to listen and hear you when you explain what helps and what doesn't. No one can learn without listening first.

Let's delve into some scenarios where we'll look at how to talk to someone who doesn't understand psychosis because of their own stigma. I'll be using the same format of answer one and answer two as I did in Chapter 2. Here's a quick recap:

- **Answer one** is for those of you who know someone with psychosis, but you haven't experienced it yourself. It's also for those of us with psychosis, but when we don't want to bring our lived experience into the discussion.
- **Answer two** is for those of us with psychosis and conversations where we feel our lived experience will affect their point of view.

If you don't have psychosis but want to speak on behalf of someone who does, I'd stick to **answer one**.

Friend:

A1: 'You don't need to feel worried or freaked out talking to someone who's experienced psychosis. They're regular people like you and me, so have a conversation, act how you would normally, and you'll see there's nothing to worry about.'

A2: 'You don't have to change the way you talk or act around me; I haven't changed – I was just ill. It might happen again in the future, but I'm here and open to any questions you have, so don't worry about saying the wrong thing.'

Family member:

A1: 'Don't let fear of saying the wrong thing stop you from talking to someone with psychosis. They'll probably be genuinely happy you want to learn more, and if you're not sure of what you should and shouldn't say, just ask! They won't be offended.'

A2: 'I am still the same person I was before I experienced psychosis. It's OK to ask questions and feel uncomfortable. I won't be angry or upset if you say the wrong thing; it means you're trying to understand, and it means you love me.'

Work colleague/college or school friend:

A1: 'A colleague/schoolmate with psychosis isn't a danger to you, and they have the ability to work/study here as well as anyone else.'

A2: 'Sometimes I experience/have experienced psychosis, but I've sought treatment and I'm capable of working/studying here. If you have questions about psychosis, just ask, and I'll try to answer them.'

Manager:

A1: 'An employee with psychosis is still able to do their job, but they might need accommodations put in place to make working here more accessible.'

A2: 'I don't experience psychosis constantly, and with support, I'm able to work. I might need accommodations to make work less stressful, such as remote working or flexible hours.'

Chapter 8
Stigma in Pop Culture

I was a teenager in the late 1990s and early 2000s, and apart from the fact that my eyebrows survived this period of time, I'm also proud that I was able to think critically about the stereotypes of psychosis I saw in pop culture. Even though I didn't have a mental illness diagnosis, I had begun to experience psychotic episodes. What I would see on television or at the cinema painted a radically different picture to what I was experiencing. I think it hindered me from understanding psychosis in two ways:

- I didn't connect the word 'psychosis' with what was happening to me, because depictions on-screen were extreme, stigmatizing, or plainly inaccurate.
- When I did see a connection, the portrayals filled me with terror that if I told anyone, I would be locked away forever.

Whereas depictions of depression and anxiety are now commonplace and often sensitively portrayed, similar examples of psychosis are very rare. Psychosis in movies is often tied to the horror genre and – spoiler – the character with psychosis is almost definitely the murderer.

It usually plays out like this…

A quiet, unassuming yet antisocial and vulnerable character becomes psychotic and descends into 'madness', probably with a murderous killing spree thrown in for good measure.

Now, how to unpick that!? As we've already seen, psychosis does not equal violence, but the stigma and misunderstanding with this trope goes far deeper. It becomes problematic when your introduction is the character acting 'crazy' during a psychotic episode. Psychosis isn't fused with someone's personality, and it doesn't make a person who they are. It's something anyone can experience for a number of reasons. When you have a chance to get to know a character, you can identify what their personality is, and it shows you that psychosis is separate from what makes up that person.

When I asked Kody about representations of psychosis in popular culture, he surprised me with an example he believed was positive, at least in some ways.

There's one that I always bring up, because I love the show – even though I think, within the show, there are a few bad examples of psychosis-related disorders. But on the show *Criminal Minds*, the mother of Spencer Reid, I think, is my favourite portrayal I've seen. She has paranoid schizophrenia. And I think the actor does a really amazing job. And I think they're very clear to really explain what's going on with her symptoms. Throughout the show, you see how she has different struggles with medication. And sometimes in the show, you'll see she's very understanding about what's going on. And then it was very similar to when I was growing up watching my mom struggling with schizophrenia. It was very similar to her experience.

I explained to Kody that I hadn't thought to ask about any positive representations, and asked him why he thought that was.

> Well, the thing is, there are so many negative ones that it's almost any other portrayal I've seen I've not been a fan of. Whereas that was the first one I watched where every time they showed this character, and she's not a main character. She's definitely a secondary character. But anytime they showed the character, I felt I was watching my mom. And so, I was like, this is, in my opinion, one of the better portrayals of schizophrenia or psychosis that I've seen.

There is some good news. UK mental health charity Mind have their own media advisory service which offers advice to producers, researchers, and writers on how to create accurate and sensitively portrayed dramatizations of mental illness in soaps and dramas. In recent years, the media advisory service has worked with soaps *EastEnders* and *Coronation Street* on storylines involving post-partum psychosis and a character's first experience of a psychotic episode.

I'm a gamer, and long before games had immersive storylines, I was trying and failing to beat the Labyrinth Zone in *Sonic* on my SEGA Mega Drive. Fast-forward, and modern games often include rich storytelling, which can go to places film and TV can't. A recent example is *Hellblade: Senua's Sacrifice*. From the title alone, it doesn't sound promising, but the portrayal of Senua's auditory hallucinations is one of the most accurate I've ever encountered. The developers invite you to play the game in headphones, so the chattering, overlapping voices can be heard all around you. Although it's in the psychological horror genre, rather than a game that focuses on psychosis as the driving force of the character, it attempts to allow the player to experience symptoms similar to psychosis.

Media representations reach millions. They can be a force for good, and media that gets it right can be a chance to put stereotypes to bed, or at least challenge misconceptions and get people thinking.

How to talk to friends and family about stigmatizing content

Step one is to explain *what part* of the content was stigmatizing.

'The movie focused on the character's psychosis, as if it was the central part of their personality.'

'Psychosis was used as a plot device for the character to go "crazy" and start murdering people.'

Step two is to explain *why* it contributes to stigma.

'Psychosis is not a personality trait. People are complex and shouldn't be defined or described by something they have no control over.'

'Only a tiny minority of people with psychosis are violent. This representation isn't accurate and perpetuates a false narrative around psychosis.'

Step three is to explain *how it affects you,* or someone you're close to with psychosis.

'It's upsetting to see psychosis depicted in this way, because I feel people will only see the psychosis when they talk to me, and not who I really am.'

'It makes me nervous to open up and tell people I have psychosis, because they might see me as a violent killer.'

Step four is to explain you're open to *any questions* they have.

'If you have any questions about psychosis, I'll try to answer as best I can.'

'I can explain more about my experiences of psychosis, if you have any questions.'

Chapter 9

Stigma in the Media

Most people have a vague idea about the word 'psychosis' or 'psychotic'. It's probably gained from the news, newspapers, or documentaries. News outlets jump on stories that involve violence, and they are often guilty of linking psychosis with violent behaviour. One example is terrorist attacks and mass shootings being blamed on the mentally ill, and, more specifically, someone suffering from psychosis. It all leads to the general public having a negative view of psychosis.

I asked Jen if she had understood what psychosis was from what she'd seen in the media before she experienced a psychotic episode aged 27.

> I probably had a negative view of psychosis in my head; I didn't really understand it. And it was something that felt so far away – I was never going to experience something like that. And then I did, and then it was something I had to grapple with.

Jen is a journalism graduate. I asked her how she feels media representation of psychosis needs to change.

I think they need to show it happens to ordinary people, like people who are very nice, very friendly, leading normal jobs, and it can happen to anyone – literally anyone. And it doesn't make you a bad person. It doesn't make you dangerous. It just makes you more vulnerable to stresses. And just make sure people are aware that it happens. It can happen to anyone really.

Michelle's view is that the news only gives people what they want – and that's bad news.

I just think the news…the news is what's in the news, right? But you turn on the 11 o'clock news… First three minutes. Somebody got slashed, somebody got robbed – that's all the first three minutes, right? You're never gonna hear, 'This person with schizophrenia woke up in the morning, had a cup of coffee. Then they went to work. After work, they met up with a friend and they went home, had dinner, and they went to sleep.' Because crisis and mental illness is public while wellness and mental illness is private. So, you're never going to hear the good stories. You will love to hear the bad stories, just like on the nightly news every day. Right? The nightly news says all the news throughout the week and then the last ten minutes on Friday, they share their great story of the week. The one good story that happened that week that they're going to share for the last ten minutes on a Friday. You don't share good news ever. You only share the bad news. Nobody is like, 'Oh, what good things are happening right now.' People only want to hear bad news. So, we only share bad news. People don't like the good stories.

Unfortunately, many people who watch/read/listen to the news – however they consume media – are watching because they want drama. They want to know the latest scandal or gossip, and when terrible events happen, their voyeuristic side is drawn to the catastrophe. News outlets know this, and as the market becomes more cramped and more saturated, they need to draw in audiences and get those clicks to their websites. When it comes to psychosis, if someone mentally ill commits a crime, it's an opportunity to create outrage and panic, both of which mean bigger audiences.

As someone who works as a freelance writer, I try to pitch personal and opinion pieces based on psychosis. It's an important topic, which doesn't get much factually accurate press. I'm used to rejection, and the 'not one for us' emails from editors, and I understand and accept why. But when I pitch an informative think piece based on negative coverage of psychosis and I get turned down because 'we've already covered this' or 'that's not newsworthy at the moment', I'm less likely to accept that reasoning. First, if psychosis isn't newsworthy now, when will it be? There shouldn't be a quota where we can only talk about it once a year or on an awareness day. I'll do some digging (this has happened on three separate occasions) and find the last piece published was over a year ago. On one occasion, it was three years since the publication had posted anything about psychosis that wasn't framed negatively. It's a frustrating experience, and one of the reasons I knew I needed to write this book and see it published.

When it comes down to it, people with psychosis are the ones explaining and giving context to psychosis. Sara, who has a diagnosis of schizophrenia, explained to me how frustrating this can feel.

I think there was a thing in the news last year, about someone who pushed someone on to a railway line. The news headline just specifically picked up on the word 'schizophrenic'. And I, as a person with that illness, can see how disgusting that is, but a lot of people won't be able to recognize why it's harmful. Like, you'll have to explain it to them in detail before they get it. And I feel like people with these illnesses shouldn't have to sit and explain. There needs to be more awareness around why news broadcasters do this and why films do it. It's to isolate a group of people who actually aren't at all what they're saying that we are.

Although the picture seems a bit grim, there are organizations out there trying to make meaningful change in how issues such as psychosis are reported on.

I asked Natasha Devon, MBE, writer, activist, broadcaster, and the founder of the Mental Health Media Charter, about the importance of responsible reporting and journalism.

Kai: What impact has the charter had on reporting and journalism in the UK?

Natasha: The idea behind the charter was to simplify some of the charity media guidelines. For example, Samaritans have some really excellent and comprehensive advice for journalists on tackling suicide stories, yet they are often not followed. We wanted to give people in media the benefit of the doubt – perhaps they're working to a deadline and don't have time to read through them. So, we boiled the media guidelines from Beat [eating disorder charity], Mental Health First Aid England, and Samaritans down to the very basics. It's seven really simple rules for writing or speaking about mental health – a kind of a 'this is the least you can do' type of thing.

Since we created the charter, more than 300 newspapers, magazines, podcasts, and blogs have signed up. In addition to the charter, we also continuously engage in work to hold the media to account. We ask our followers to alert us when media reporting is misleading or stigmatizing, and we create discussion around the piece, correct the errors, and (where appropriate/possible) ask for a retraction, edit, or apology.

We are a very small group of volunteers, so our reach and capacity to bring about change isn't as broad as we'd like, but we're incredibly passionate about ensuring mental health reporting is educational, informative, and doesn't increase stigma. We're proud to have created an online space where our followers can talk about where media reporting gets it wrong and advocate for those who have been harmed.

Kai: What more do you feel needs to be done in the media to educate and eradicate stigma?

Natasha: I believe the mental health conversation needs more specificity. When I'm not working with the Mental Health Media Charter, I do work in schools and colleges all over the world. I deliver talks and conduct research on mental health issues in the 'middle layer' – i.e. not mental illnesses, but things which impact wellbeing and can affect a young person's ability to function. These include exam stress, body image insecurity, social media addiction, and navigating life transitions.

When people discuss these types of issues, they either pathologize them and make them sound as though they are the same as diagnosable mental illness, or they go the other way and start talking about stiff upper lips and young people needing to have more 'resilience'. Neither of these is right.

We need to start thinking of mental health in terms of a spectrum and mental health issues as things that get progressively worse over time if the person experiencing them isn't given the support they need to manage them.

Another area where specificity would be useful is where

crimes have been committed – particularly terrorist offences. Saying 'the terrorist had mental health issues' (a) is vague and (b) throws those with diagnosed mental illnesses under the bus by presenting them all as potentially dangerous. That's why in the charter we ask journalists to flag when this is based on speculation and to emphasize that mental illness alone doesn't cause terrorism.

I also wish journalists would understand that something having just been acknowledged is not the same as it having massively increased. Mental health issues aren't new, but they weren't discussed or measured in the same way historically. That doesn't mean 'suddenly everyone is mentally ill' (as is often implied). It simply means people now have the knowledge and nomenclature to more accurately express what they're going through.

What can I do if I see stigmatizing content from news outlets and media?

In the UK, if you see content that's harmful and stereotypical of psychosis, you can report it to the Independent Press Standards Organisation (IPSO) as a complaint. As of right now, IPSO only looks at content that is harmful towards an individual rather than a group of people with a disability. Alternatively, you can contact the Mental Health Media Charter or take your complaint directly to the publication. The more people who complain, the more likely someone will sit up and take notice. A few organizations you can contact:

- Impress (UK) – www.impressorg.com
- Ethical Journalism Network (International) – https://ethicaljournalismnetwork.org
- Society of Professional Journalists (US) – www.spj.org

Don't click. We've all done it, and we've all regretted it: we've all fallen for clickbait. If you see a stigmatizing headline about psychosis, don't click through to the article. If you do click through, screenshot and share the article so others don't need to click but can still report it or complain. If fewer people read these articles, the media outlets will be less likely to publish them.

Write, or create, or video your own counter-post – either through social media, an open letter, or pitch a story to a news outlet.

Chapter 10
Social Media

There's been much reporting on how social media negatively affects your general mental health. Social media isn't just for doom scrolling, but it's also rife with misinformation, bad medical takes, and stigmatizing content. If you're starting from the ground floor, it can be difficult to push aside the falsehoods blocking the elevator to reveal the truth. And that's the case for psychosis.

A few years ago, I worked as a barista. I had occasional shifts in a shop on a busy main road. One morning, I noticed a woman shouting outside on the street. She was screaming at the top of her voice, and most of what she was saying didn't make sense. She sounded confused and distressed. My first thought was that she must be ill and going through some sort of mental health crisis. The woman was confronted by police and tried to get away. She was restrained and then taken away by three police officers. It was a distressing sight to witness. I explained what had happened on the work WhatsApp group and the response was 'Did you film it?!' When I said no, I hadn't filmed a woman in distress without her consent, the next response jokingly told me off for not doing it and encouraged me to film it 'next time'. It was an extreme example of how we're dehumanized when we're psychotic. Social media can bring out the worst in us, especially when we're motivated by likes and comments and constant external validation.

Social media is a minefield, especially if you're honest about psychosis.

I asked Sara if she'd had a lot of pushback from people when she'd tried to explain what they're saying on social media about psychosis is not OK.

> Yeah, I'd say more so in person, people are more willing to be open about it. But I'd say on environments like Twitter/X, for example, I've had many arguments. Some people just are not willing to understand where you're coming from. And I think sometimes it can get skewed, obviously, because you can't detect people's tones, or why they were speaking in a certain way. But I definitely say more with conversations I've had in person. I think if you just explain how it makes you feel, it can almost bring them down a level, so they don't get so defensive, because that's what a lot of people do – they're right, you're wrong. And they just jump to being defensive if they feel they're being criticized. But I think if you just try and be like, 'Well, look, this is how this makes me feel' and then go about it from that, they can be a bit less likely to kick off about it.

Online mental health advocacy can be problematic. The name, for starters. It doesn't make sense to advocate for all mental health, and many people, like me, instead call themselves advocates for better understanding of mental illness, not mental health in general.

It's almost as if this sphere of the internet has become yet another type of influencer. It's become skewed and disjointed during the time I've been an advocate, which I started back in 2012. And I don't believe an advocate should ever be an influencer. Hear me out. Because then it all becomes about the way you carry yourself and the way you present yourself on social media and how you want people to perceive you. If you have a mental illness, things are messy and raw. You can't be perfect. I look at some feeds and even the messiness looks orchestrated and sanitized. It's the whole 'perfectly imperfect' vibe. It doesn't work because the two won't mesh together.

Chris has struggled with having a large following on social media, where he shares his experiences of psychosis through his artwork.

I really hate when people deify, or they try to make my stuff cult-like or weird. People ask the creepiest questions, I swear. I've had people call me the devil and they mean it. Like this is Satan's work. And then I've had people who were religious sending nasty things about, like, 'Who do you think you are?' Or like, 'My brother has schizophrenia and he's not like you.' And it's like, 'I never said I was like your brother.'

I asked Chris if it felt as if people were saying, 'You can't have that experience because mine is different.'

Well, yeah, that's what the Reddit posts about me say. Where they're all like, 'This guy's fake' or 'My schizophrenia is way worse than his.' And I'm like, 'What? What the hell? Who are you people? It's not a competition.' The only person I'm competing with is me. Every day.

With social media, we're opening ourselves up to millions of people around the world. With that comes an array of opinions, life experience, and deep-rooted stigma of mental illness. When you have a big following or have a post which goes viral out the blue, it can feel overwhelming. I take regular breaks from social media, because it's the best way I've found to protect my mental health. I know if I showed up daily, I'd be more popular and have a larger following. In my mind, it's not worth the risk to my health. I'd rather stay stable and contented than playing the social media game every single day.

I've met some wonderful people through social media, people I now regard as close friends. But I've also had some really horrible experiences. I just don't like how performative it is. Often when someone's trying to drag you down, it's a performance. They want to show off, and they want to show why they're right and you're wrong in the loudest, most theatrical way possible.

A massive problem with social media is the lack of nuance. Talking about a complicated subject like psychosis online means your views and well-thought-out points can be easily misconstrued. Some conversations really do work better face to face.

Anonymity is another enormous problem on social media. Libby explains how people can say awful things which they wouldn't say face to face.

There's so many problems I have with social media, and how a lot of people say they care so much about people's wellbeing. They actually don't. Because they say things. And I think to myself, you would never come up to me and say that, ever. I don't understand this whole thing of a computer screen giving people confidence that they wouldn't have normally. And it's not the right kind of confidence. I think a lot of the time, you could even just have it in a private chat. At the moment, I feel people get this kind of 'something' from humiliating others. Because there are so many things that definitely can be said privately. But they won't. I don't know what they get from it, but they get something from it. I've never understood that. And I don't think I ever will. I have a very, very mixed relationship with social media. It's caused me a huge amount of trauma. But it's also been very positive.

I think people don't want to admit when they're wrong, either. I've definitely been guilty of jumping on bandwagons when other people have dogpiled. I've been hurt by a situation. And I guess, other people doing it has made me feel like this is my chance to speak about it as well. A few days or weeks later, I've thought I didn't actually need to do that. That could have been done privately. And it just didn't need to happen. You get so caught up in social media. It's a strange one. I try to use it more for personal use. Especially Instagram. I try to post things that make me happy, rather than constantly feeling pressure to post perfect stuff. I think, 'Do I want to share this with the world?' And if it's yes, 'Is it because it makes me happy?' And if that's a yes, then I post it.

How to look after yourself on social media

When we see something stigmatizing about psychosis on social media, for many of us, our first response is anger. Although it feels good in the moment, an angry comment isn't always helpful or warranted. People often live in their echo chamber, full of voices with similar experiences and opinions, which amplify one another. When they step out by posting on social media and are faced with aggression, then all we're doing is helping them prove their point. It's fine to be angry about a cause you care about, but how we use that anger matters.

Kody works as a mental health advocate and has had to learn how to take care of himself online.

My entire career has become mental health advocacy. And so I'm in a position where getting defensive isn't going to help anyone. I'm in a position where, as a person who's well known now for being someone with schizophrenia, and who has a rather big following, I have found myself trying as hard as possible to educate instead of shame people, because no one's going to change their point of view if you try to make them feel bad for what they said. I've found that me educating people to the best of my abilities, and then letting them go from there, some people are going to be willing to learn, some people are not. And so I just stick to providing education about whatever the topic is. A lot of the time, I do have resources I provide to people, NAMI (National Alliance on Mental Illness) is a really popular one I give to people, and Mental Health America. There are plenty of resources for people to learn about psychosis or schizophrenia. And so I just find myself providing them with the resources to get the education they need on the topic, if that's what they decide to do.

I have a couple of videos going viral on Instagram right now. So my comments are more full than usual with a lot of very stigmatized statements. Anytime I have videos doing really well, it's not just my followers who are seeing it whenever it makes it to the other side of platforms where people aren't following me or aren't aware of my story. That's where I start seeing a lot that misconception coming through.

I asked Kody how he looks after himself online.

I just try to separate myself as needed; I will block someone in a heartbeat if I feel like they're trying to cause me any sort of issues with my symptoms. I'm also very good at knowing I need to take time away from social media. So I try to avoid social media if I feel I need to step away, which I was really bad at initially, but I found I have to do it if I want to worry about my own and prioritize my own mental health.

So how can we look after ourselves on social media?

- **Set daily limits.** We all know social media can be addictive, and we're all guilty of being drawn into long, drawn-out arguments which wind us up and make us feel crap. Set yourself a daily limit and stick to it. Try other activities away from your phone.
- **Join smaller social media groups.** Every social media platform works differently, and it's possible to curate a smaller group of like-minded people if you find some platforms too overwhelming or confrontational. It can also be a welcome break if you want to stay active across social media platforms. Sites like Mastodon and Discord work well if you want a more positive and supportive social media experience.
- **Mute, block, and report stigmatizing content.** If you see content that is misleading, hateful, or abusive, you should report it right away. Even if the post or video stays up, you're giving the moderators and developers a better picture of what is and isn't acceptable to their users. Muting and blocking also keep you safe, especially if someone is being abusive or just won't get the hint and refuses to move on. It's also a good idea to make your social media accounts private, even temporarily, if you feel overwhelmed.
- **Walk away.** When I want to rant and rave, I physically put down my phone and walk away. I'll take some deep breaths, go and make a drink, put the washing on,

whatever inane chore I need to do – anything other than commenting something hateful back. It works, and the next time I pick up my phone, if I still feel the need to reply, my comment is calmer, more measured, and better informed.

- **Stay calm and rational.** This is easier said than done! But it works when you're trying to educate someone online. People act differently on social media to how they would in real life, and are quicker to feel provoked, insulted, and patronized. When we lose our temper, the other person will believe they've 'won' the debate, or your comments prove their stigmatized view. Staying calm and sticking to a rational argument is disarming – you're not adding any fuel to the fire, and it forces the other person to do the same, or they end up looking irrational and argumentative. Staying calm and rational also gives more validity to any point you're hoping to make.

- **Educate and inform.** This can be by sharing your lived experience to show how their view is misinformed or by sharing some myth-busting facts about psychosis. Educating others is the most powerful tool you have for combating misrepresentations and stigma.

- **Move on.** Sometimes, the only thing we can do is move on. When faced with a barrage of deeply stigmatizing comments from an individual, it can become obvious very quickly that you're never going to get anywhere. The only choice is to leave it and move on. It's not a case of losing an argument or debate, because really it was one-sided all along. The person you've been messaging never wanted to learn or understand your point of view. It's better to spend your time and energy on people who are open to learning and challenging their stigmatized views.

- **Pick your battles.** It's important to remember that your voice is just as vital and needed as the person who seemingly has it all together. Sometimes moving on is the right thing to do, but then, sometimes, standing your ground is the best move. It's all about picking your battles. Understand the times when someone won't or refuses to listen and how they differ from those moments when you can see someone is willing to learn and genuinely wants to know your point of view.

We can all play a part in making social media a more positive and healthier place to be. We can support people who do share content about severe mental illness and psychosis and share what they have to say. We can all lift up marginalized voices and give them the space and platform to share their stories, give their opinions, and explain when something isn't working and what we can all do for the better.

People will often shy away from connecting with people who have a severe mental illness. It might be a lack of understanding and education that stops them. The media then has a responsibility to highlight what makes people uncomfortable and address it. Rather than creating articles, publishing books, and making podcasts that they know will be popular, take a chance and be on the side of those who feel isolated and invisible. Mindfulness is a trend; it's a fad. When it fades into the background and out of the public consciousness, what's left? Psychosis will still be here. There will still be people fighting a battle every day. You might disagree with me, but these trends happen in cycles.

I think we all can often live in a bubble. A bubble full of supportive, like-minded people on social media. When that bubble inevitably pops, we see what public perceptions of severe mental illness are really like. It's important that we have these difficult conversations with people who disagree with us or are peddling stigmatizing tropes about mental illness. It doesn't need to be a confrontation if we look at it from a different point of view to our own.

I have struggled with the idea of my work not being popular. That it isn't relatable enough. Sometimes I think I would have more readers, make more money, and have an easier time of it if I wrote more about general wellbeing. That if I pitched more articles about this, I'd have more commissions as a freelancer. But I don't. I'm authentic and write honestly and truthfully. The moment I stopped comparing myself to others and thought, 'Fuck it, I'll do this my way', I found writing and social media much more therapeutic and enjoyable.

If you see someone taking a chance and writing about severe mental illness, support them. Like and comment on their content. Share their stories. If you see someone peeping over the parapet and writing in the press about psychosis or schizophrenia, for instance, read what they have to say. Especially articles written by ethnic minorities and those from the LGBTQ+ community.

Again, share it far and wide and encourage others to read and learn about severe mental illness. Please don't ignore us. We can be a vital part of the mental health conversation.

Chapter 11

Medical Professionals, Mental Health Services, and Prison Services

Sometimes stigma comes from the very services whose care and support we need when we're at our most vulnerable. Unfortunately, if you have psychosis, you may encounter stigma from medical professionals. There's also a disproportionate number of people with psychosis and severe mental illness in general in prison.

Hazel told me about how they're trying to work with a hospital to help them better understand the patients who present with psychosis.

I'm currently working with the hospital trying to sort this nonsense out. I had scars on my legs before psychosis was even on my record. So, when I said to the doctor 'Can you check that the tracking device has definitely gone?' they just sent me home. And this was three, four years before anyone noticed I had psychosis. I'm gonna say it could have been picked up so much earlier! It really annoys me.

I don't know why it happened. I don't know if they misunderstood what I was trying to say. I don't know if they just didn't want to deal with it that day. There have been times when I've eaten or drunk things I shouldn't because I thought it might break the tracker, and I've ended up in A&E [accident and emergency] for that as well. And they've put it down as self-poisoning. And it's OK, technically. But also no. I think part of it is because I've been on loads and loads of training things about suicide, self-harm, mental illness, etc., and psychosis is very rarely mentioned. So I think it might be a training issue. I think the doctors just don't know. They might think I'm just taking the piss or something. They don't realize it's actually a thing and that they should probably flag it up.

If you're training to be a doctor, and unless you're specializing in psychiatry, it's a tiny part of the course. It's real basics.

In the UK, during the training for General Practitioner Speciality Trainees (GPST), students have one opportunity to choose a mental health placement, through a placement in psychiatry. According to a 2017 survey by UK charity Mind, 'Of GPs across the country who completed training in 2017, 46% completed a psychiatry placement.' However, GPs surveyed also wanted further training: '72% would like more Continuing Professional Development (CPD) training related to mental health' (Mind 2018).

In the US, the training time for medical students on mental health is about 5.1 weeks (even less in residencies), which is about 2.5 per cent of total medical school and residency training time (Smith 2020).

When you think about everything mental health covers, and the depth and breadth of different mental illnesses, imagine now how little time is devoted to psychosis.

Kody spoke to me about his experiences of the criminal justice system.

I also struggled with addiction, incarceration. I feel like I dealt with a lot of stigma in the criminal justice system. I also noticed that police interactions when I was first struggling with my mental illness, and I was undiagnosed, usually did not go well, because they weren't trained to adequately deal with someone with serious mental illness. Police were trained to treat serious mental illness as either crime or drug use. I feel like a lot of the stigma I dealt with was from people within the criminal justice system, police officers, and then employers a little bit early on, like I said, more so because I didn't have a diagnosis and I wasn't getting any form of treatment at the time.

Roughly half of prisoners in the United States have concerns related to mental health and up to 25 per cent have a serious mental illness (bipolar, schizophrenia, etc.) (American Psychological Association 2014). Eighty-five per cent of the prison population have an active substance use disorder or were incarcerated for a crime involving drugs or drug use (National Institute on Drug Abuse 2020).

In England and Wales, 48 per cent of men and 70 per cent of women in prison experience mental health 'problems' (HM Inspectorate of Probation 2021) and 8 per cent of prisoners have a diagnosis of psychosis (National Collaborating Centre for Mental Health 2021).

Mental illnesses and psychosis are often worsened by prison, and not all staff have the training to understand mental illness and trauma. Ultimately, we need to stop criminalizing mental illness and start getting people the help they need. This could involve making sure people can access mental health care in the community, investing in community services which give people with psychosis a place to go and meet other people, and sign-posting to other services that can offer support and guidance. People with psychosis should not have to go to prison for their own protection, but instead receive care in hospital or in the community. Nobody should be punished for something that is out of their control, like psychosis.

Sara has noticed that when she's needed to go to the emergency department because of a psychotic episode, she is treated differently by staff compared to other patients.

I think I noticed that more. If I'm in crisis, or anytime I've gone to an A&E department or phoned for an ambulance or things like that, they'll triage you and they'll look at your records. Every single time, they've looked at the fact that I've got a schizophrenia diagnosis, they call the police, and they say it's a safety issue. And I think for me, like some people will be like, 'Well, it is just in case, to keep you safe.' But I don't think they understand how terrifying it is to be in crisis and so paranoid about everything around you and then have the people who are supposed to be helping you act as if you're a threat or you're gonna hurt someone. It's something that I've tried to explain to a lot of people why it's stigmatizing. Why they look at what medication you're on or your experiences and go, 'I know, this is what we'll do.' And I've had a situation where I was in crisis and went to A&E, and I've been there for so long waiting that I felt fine again. If you've been waiting for six hours, by that time (sometimes) it's passed, and you're fine. I'd gone in voluntarily and I said, 'Look, they've not seen me yet, I'm absolutely fine. I'm safe to leave, I'll get a friend to pick me up and take me home', and they said, 'No, we'll have to phone the police and they'll probably come to your house. And if you don't answer, then they can knock your door down.' And that was what they said to me. And I was, like, how is that an appropriate thing to say to somebody? Like, I just don't understand how someone can – it's like they're just not understanding, especially if you're already paranoid. You're then like, 'Oh, my God, why? Why would they? Why would they do that to me? What have I done wrong?' You are feeling guilty for just wanting to get support.

I've had it probably the last six times I've been. I always noticed that in medical settings, particularly because I think a lot of people think that, with psychosis, you're destined to just be drugged and hospitalized. And I just think it's such a horrible thing to think about people because you shouldn't have to, like drugging somebody and putting them in hospital is almost isolating them from society and expecting that's how they should exist. I really struggle with it. Because I don't like this idea that people with psychosis have to be medicated. I think it's a choice. It should never be something that's forced on you.

Yeah, it's a massive thing [lack of training]. I think a lot of them haven't had much at all, and then don't know how to respond to people. I think the lack of specialist services and care that there is for people with a more complex diagnosis, I think that's a real problem. So I think most people will have an understanding of depression and anxiety and how to treat those, but they don't have any understanding of more complex things. And I've always found it difficult to navigate mental health care in this country, because it is so tailored to specific things, and they just don't know how to respond to you.

In order for change to happen, more voices of people with psychosis need to be heard by medical professionals. If you're able, lived-experience roles, either paid or voluntary, can help shape policy in hospitals and in general practice. Even getting in touch with a hospital or general practitioner with feedback about your experience of the care you received can make a difference.

An example of good care would involve:

- an understanding that there isn't a one-size-fits-all solution to psychosis
- treating individuals with empathy
- treating individuals with respect and dignity
- using active listening skills and hearing and understanding what works for the individual
- implementing strategies the individual knows has worked in the past
- understanding that someone with psychosis is an expert by lived experience
- understanding that someone who is psychotic is not automatically a danger to others
- following any crisis plan the individual has put together and respecting their decisions
- understanding that someone with psychosis is vulnerable and needs support and compassion
- using restraint (physical or chemical) as a very last resort and only by trained professionals
- understanding that restraint can be traumatic.

Chapter 12

Language Matters

Language is a powerful tool of expression. We tell stories with language, and these stories conjure up images and ideas in the listener. We can change the way people think or perceive the world around them with the language we use. Language can change people's opinions of others and, more importantly, when it comes to mental health and illness, themselves.

Is it really such a big deal?

If you throw around the words 'psychotic' or 'delusional' to describe someone you disagree with or roll it out when you've been hurt or upset, then you can't call yourself a mental health advocate or say that you care about mental illness. There, I've said it.

The misuse of these words is one of those things about mental illness that just doesn't stick when you talk about it. People don't want to change the language they use, don't see it's a problem, or simply forget the point and start using the words all over again.

I see or hear the word 'psychotic' misused pretty much every day. It's either on social media, in TV or film, or in passing when I'm out in public, and even from friends and family. So really, it's *everywhere*. It's exhausting to keep calling it out or getting annoyed at a show or a movie or even a friend when they use it in the wrong context.

I've had people say to me, 'C'mon, it's not a big deal, it's just a word!'

It's important to listen to the opinion of people who are actually psychotic. Who live with the condition/symptom and have to hear the word negatively used every single day. Imagine you've been diagnosed with psychosis. The word 'psychotic' has become a part of your life, whether you want it to or not. You know the feeling of dread when you start to hear, see, or feel things that aren't really there. You remember the extreme paranoia or delusions of grandeur that come with delusional thinking. You're slowly learning to manage it, but it's terrifying. It's confusing and disorientating. It makes you feel extremely vulnerable. You feel untethered from reality and as if there is no safety net to catch you. Because of all of this, you're at a higher risk when you're ill of being the victim of violence than the general population. Later that day, you find a show you think you'll like and put it on the telly. The villain, the character the audience is supposed to hate, is described as psychotic. The next day, a family member rants to you about a politician. They tell you that they're 'evil, dangerous, psychotic'. And it continues like this, with people all around you casually throwing the word around – not once thinking about the impact it will have on you.

Then there's the crowd who will say:

'But what about freedom of speech!'

'Stop policing my language!'

We all have freedom of speech, because we're allowed to use the word 'psychotic' in any way we'd like. Nobody can stop anyone else from using language the way they want. But freedom of speech goes both ways. As much as someone is allowed to use words in a certain way, people are allowed to not like it. The difference from say, 15, 20 years ago, is people are now more vocal. People like me didn't feel they could talk about the way certain words were used, but as society is now more open about mental health in general, we feel that we can now make ourselves heard.

As for policing language, controlling and regulating language is very different to somebody expressing a concern or explaining how the use of a word is harmful and damaging. What people are unhappy about are consequences. When we're rude or offensive, we face consequences, and that's true for every action we take.

It gets complicated with language. People feel we are trying to tell them what to do or telling them what they're not allowed to say. They get offended by it. Really, all we're asking for is just common decency.

All I'm asking is for people to think before they speak. It all adds up. It might not seem like a big deal, but hearing these words constantly misused takes its toll. If you live with psychosis, it warps the way you think about yourself. You start questioning:

'Am I a bad person?'

'Am I dangerous when I'm ill?'

'Am I evil?'

Because the word has been given a different meaning by the people around you and in society in general, it's so commonly misused that you start to doubt whether the way you use the word is right. It grinds you down, it makes you feel like you're broken, and people see you as dangerous.

'I'm not worth anyone's time or energy.'

'Maybe I deserve to be treated this way.'

'I must be a nasty piece of work for people to talk like that.'

They're not 'just words'; they carry venom that poisons people who are already vulnerable. It stops people from accessing care and support because they don't want the label. It isolates people who already feel alone and misunderstood.

By using these terms, all you're doing is insinuating our symptoms are synonymous with badness.

Sara told me how she feels when 'psychotic' and 'delusional' are misused.

> God, I can't describe the sort of anger I feel whenever I see it misused. It's so common, especially 'delusional'. I've constantly seen 'psychotic' as well. Even just calling politicians and stuff psychotic. I can't, it just fills my body with rage! I just want everyone to know why it's wrong. And you can't because it's exhausting. And you can't pull up every single person who says it because it's so misused. And again, I think that a massive part of that is down to the lack of education about psychosis. The reasons that people think it's all right to use language like that when they're misusing it is, it just gets me down so much.

The difficulty is that it's constant. In the modern world, we're bombarded with media, more than ever before. When words related to psychosis are misused over and over, it's upsetting to witness. It feels almost personal, and it can feel an exhausting process to let people know why it's wrong and why it's damaging for you. It's so ingrained in our language that it can feel overwhelming to challenge. No one should be expected to constantly have to pull people up on their choice of words. It's an impossible task. Sara explains how talking about it affects her.

> I think if I've seen friends use it, I'll speak to them about it. And they'll be like, 'Oh, God, I'm so sorry, I didn't even realize.' But, sometimes people will push back and go, 'It's just a word.' And it's like, you're not understanding. That word is so heavily charged; it has so much motive behind it. And they don't understand the violence and stigma that people with psychosis face because of those words being used against them as well. So yeah, it enrages me.

To go back to an earlier story, I once heard someone describe an ex: 'He was terrible. Horrible. He was a psychotic Nazi.'

I was so shocked at the time that I didn't question why they'd used the word in this way. When we use language negatively, we're conflating psychosis with a group of people who committed abhorrent crimes. This then just adds to the stigma and stereotypes, and we're left with a bigger problem to try to combat.

Libby explained how she feels about the inaccurate use of language and her internal struggle with how she uses language.

> I think frustrated more than anything. I used to get really upset by it. Especially 'psycho', the abbreviation of 'psychotic' – a psycho, which used to really bother me. And I used to get really upset by those kinds of things. But now I just get frustrated that people are just not listening. But then I get frustrated at myself. Because even sometimes myself, I do it. I think why have I just

done that? I know that's not OK. And I think it's just these terms – we've used them for so long that it takes time even for you to unlearn them yourself. I'm very black and white and very literal, so sometimes I think of the context of what would that mean by a textbook dictionary definition. And sometimes I'm like, 'Well, technically, they're not using the term wrong.' And then I get annoyed at myself, because I think, 'Yes, but it's the context they're using it, Libby!' So even with myself, sometimes I have to check myself and be like, 'Stop thinking so literally. People are using these terms in derogatory ways. Not everyone thinks the way you do.' So, then I think, how mad can I get at other people? If even I do it sometimes? I try not to get upset by it anymore. I try to remember, most of the time people are using it in a derogatory way, not the way that I use it. So, I try to educate them and say, 'You really shouldn't be saying that.' And some people are really open to that. Some people are like, 'Oh, what's wrong with it? Why can't I say it?' And some people are like, 'It's not that deep, stop making a big deal out of nothing.' And I'm like, 'Well, it's not nothing, is it?' Often when it gets to that point, I'm like, 'We'll save this conversation for another day.'

Kody explains how he doesn't see the point in getting upset with people, but how by staying calm and rational, he usually receives a more positive response.

I go back to just educating because that's what I'm used to. That's what I ended up doing. With being a person who's an advocate, I ended up just always resorting to educating by any means. So I found getting upset about it, once again, isn't going to change anyone's mind. If I can try to educate people on why I believe those terms are important to be used in the correct scientific medical standard way, I think people are more willing to take it and consider it, instead of me just getting upset. And people being like, 'Oh, you all get upset about everything these days', I found I get a lot better response if I can actually explain to people why I believe those terms should be used specifically for their medical purpose.

It's important to explain to people the difference in how language is used. For instance, 'delusional' does have a regular meaning, but when it's targeted at a person who is struggling or used in a negative way to make fun of someone or demean them, then it crosses the line to stigmatizing.

There's only one definition of what psychotic is, but people still use it in a derogatory way, as it's used colloquially to explain when someone is wrong, they've acted in a terrible way, or an idea is ridiculous.

'Psycho' is where it gets complicated. Some people use the term as an abbreviation of 'psychopath' but when other people use it, they're thinking of psychotic.

Sam has noticed how language is misused in pop culture and the media.

I noticed the word 'psychosis' used inaccurately everywhere now. I started keeping track of it and they mentioned it offhand as an insult or to mark out something as bad. It's the subtle mentions I'm not expecting that sometimes get to me most. 'I'm just trying to watch the telly, stop stigmatizing me.'

Hazel spoke to me about how their point of view has changed regarding language and psychosis.

I didn't used to [worry about language] but then I started thinking, when they're using it in that way, that's what they're thinking of me. So it bothers me now. And language has always been one that didn't really bother me all that much. But the more I've been involved in the anti-stigma stuff, and the advocacy, the more I started realizing it does have an effect. It does permeate into society, and also the way they see us in general. It also sort of devalues the word almost and belittles our real, genuine issues.

They even use it to almost dehumanize a person. Because people are so proud of the fact that we are a higher-thinking species. And that's what makes us different from the animals. And when you lose the ability to think rationally, or think logically, people then see you as either being a child or less than human in some way. Which isn't great. We're still human.

With the rise in disinformation and alternative facts, I've heard more and more people use the word 'delusional' as a slur. I've even had someone from my extended family use it, when they know I suffer with delusions. When opposing sides are arguing, or even just having a debate on an issue, the go-to word seems to be 'delusional'. I've heard phrases in the media, by experts in their field, by politicians in interviews all along the lines of...

'This policy is delusional.'

'What they're suggesting is delusional.'

'This delusion will harm the public/economy/our country, etc.'

Jen explained how difficult it is for her to hear people use the word 'delusional' in this way.

I find that really annoying because delusions are so serious and they stop people from living a normal life. And it's obvious the politician isn't delusional in the mentally ill sense, and it's such a throwaway word – people use it all the time to describe politicians. And it's just really annoying because delusions ruined my life. They were the worst, lowest point in my life, and to call a politician delusional when they're clearly not, it's just really infuriating.

It's insensitive, lazy, and a gross misuse of the word. 'But delusional means different things!' It may do, but it's obvious what meaning people are trying to convey when they call someone delusional when they deeply disagree with someone. It's hard enough trying to explain what delusions are to family and friends, without them constantly hearing the word in a negative light on the news, on social media, and from the people running our country. The more people hear the word used in this way, the more likely they are to use it in their day-to-day language.

It's just a word!

'Why does it matter what words people use? It's just a word, isn't it?'

Well, it portrays delusions and psychosis, and the people who experience them, as bad. It fuels the idea that people who experience delusions are dangerous. It's deeply hurtful to the individuals who experience psychosis. We're human beings and are affected by an illness that can completely overwhelm us and cause damage to our relationships and our lives. We deserve to be listened to when we say a word used in this negative context is hurtful.

Changing up your vocabulary isn't difficult. Try using words to convey how you feel about what someone has suggested, such as:

- unrealistic
- fantasy
- pipe dream
- confused
- wrong
- ignorant.

Think about that difference of opinion, and the emotion or belief which first pops into your head, and use that word.

I think the way 'delusional' is used shows that stigma, and a lack of knowledge and understanding, is still rife when it comes to certain mental illnesses. The less palatable it seems, the more stigma exists.

Not everyone I interviewed had the same opinion as me about language. We're all sensitive to different aspects of stigma, and language, although important, doesn't have the same emotional impact for everyone. Chris explained how he doesn't pay it any attention anymore.

I don't see it as negative any more. It's just it is what it is. Right? But what I noticed when someone uses terms like that is that they're just so uninformed, uneducated, or they just don't care. And so, I don't give attention. I just don't care. But I do give attention to the curious. Even if they don't use the right language, I'm not the first person to jump on them and attack. I know that people express themselves in different ways. And sometimes it's not always fun. But you'll learn from it, though. You learn how to deal with people over time.

When people are challenged about their use of language, they believe it's a new idea. Change is difficult, but society is constantly evolving and always has done. It's the way humans work.

However, the misuse of the words 'psychotic' and 'delusional' isn't new. Personally, I've struggled with hearing these words used offensively for nearly 20 years. Why? Because I've experienced psychosis for 20 years. Even before I was diagnosed, it would put me on edge. I've not just decided overnight that I don't want people to use the word I've been offended by for decades, but it's only recently that I've felt able to speak up and say something because society is changing. I have that platform where I can say 'No, that's not OK' and explain why.

It's not that these people never existed. They're not jumping on a bandwagon or looking for attention. It's just more people are being honest. And so more people feel able to open up as a result.

'They're mental.'   *'That's crazy/insane.'*

'What a psycho!'   *'They're so psychotic.'*

They are a myriad of words you can use to describe a situation or person. It doesn't have to have anything to do with mental illness.

Alternative words and phrases to 'psychotic', 'delusional', or 'psycho' include:

'unbelievable' *'messed up'*   *'unrealistic'*   *'ludicrous'*

'shocking'   *'outrageous'*   *'fucked up'*   *'foolish'.*

'absurd'   *'ridiculous'*   *'fanciful'*

'awful'   *'laughable'*

There are many more. I'm a firm believer in using the actual adjective you mean when describing something.

How to talk to someone about their use of language

Let's look at how to navigate difficult conversations about language. I've put together a few common questions and statements people make about this topic, and possible answers which calmly and rationally explain your point of view.

'I don't understand why it's such a big deal?'

'It might not feel like a big deal to you, but you need to understand it matters to me. It's upsetting and demoralizing to hear these words used negatively, and I hear them every day. I want people to understand it makes me feel isolated and alone, and has a massive impact on my mental health. When people don't hear me when I talk about this issue, it makes me feel worthless and that my feelings aren't as important as the language you use.'

'Why are you so upset? It's just a word!'

'It's more than just a word. It carries some very harmful connotations which could cause me/someone with psychosis to be stigmatized in a damaging way or even be a victim of violence.'

'Why should I have to change the way I talk?'

'I'm not telling you or trying to control the way you think or speak. You have the freedom and the choice to use language how you want, but I also have the freedom to tell you when I find the language you use offensive. I've explained how when you use the word 'psychotic'/'delusional' in that way, it's extremely upsetting and stigmatizing; it's your choice to continue or not to use it in that way.'

Kody talked about how he discusses with people who misuse language as part of his advocacy work.

> It's usually just me referring to why the word 'psychotic' is used, how it's used in more than medical standards, and talking about my own experience with the psychotic break. And then I found sharing personal experience helps, because then they can see why I feel so deeply about it. And that usually helps people. If you have lived experience, I think it helps them identify why you would be uncomfortable with the word being used in a negative way.

Lived experience is so impactful. And honestly, I think it's one of the most important things for breaking down stigma. You can give someone an idea of what psychosis is, but until they meet someone, talk to someone, and go, 'Oh, you're a regular person,' they won't understand.

I spoke to Jen about how important empathy is when we think about how we use language.

> You have to explain to people you can't use 'delusional' in that way. Delusions are a really serious mental illness. And you can't use it in such a throwaway way. It's not just the word to them.

Ultimately, it's all about empathy. When we throw around words and phrases because we have no problem with them, it's easy to forget how someone, or an entire group of people, can be negatively affected by our choices. Empathy is about seeing from another's point of view. It's about trying to understand how somebody else feels beyond our own opinions and reasoning. And it is a choice. No one is forcing anyone to change their use of language. What they're asking is for people to show some empathy and understanding, and to think about why a word might be offensive.

When people say there isn't much stigma left surrounding mental health, I always direct them back to how we all use language. How it's ingrained in our colloquialisms to call someone 'psychotic' or 'psycho'. How casually these terms are used, and the lack of thought that goes into what we're saying. How using these words affects how those with mental illnesses are treated. Using these words so negatively keeps the people that need help hidden.

Language is a powerful tool. Use it sensitively and with love.

PART III
HOW TO
LIVE WELL

L iving well with psychosis is hard, but it's not impossible. Part III focuses on just that, and how loved ones can support you to live well and look after yourself. We'll be diving into how to actually talk about psychosis without the 'reach out' platitudes, as well as how we can manage stress and sleep, the importance of routine, and how distractions can help keep us safe. Creating a crisis plan is integral for us, our loved ones, and our mental health team, so we'll be focusing on planning for a crisis too. The interviewees have all shared what works for them, and I offer some tips and advice from my own experience.

Living well with psychosis is no easy feat, and the advice in here is not foolproof. Mix and match what works for you, because just as the ways we experience psychosis are different, how we manage it will vary too. What works for one person will not work for everyone. It can sometimes feel like trial and error trying to figure out what causes a psychotic episode and what to do about it. From managing stress to building a routine, it takes time to create something that works for you.

Part III is also for people who want to support and help a loved one with psychosis. We'll be looking at what to do to help if you have someone in your life with psychosis.

I wanted to end the book on a positive note, and with that in mind, the interviewees and I have shared a moment of support which was significant and impactful.

Chapter 13
Staying Safe and Looking After Yourself

The problem with 'reaching out'

I often find that stressing the importance of openness and honesty means you can't move forward without sharing your story with the people closest you. It's OK to show vulnerability, and by doing all of this, we're defying stigma. But I always stop short of ever telling anyone to 'reach out'.

Telling someone to reach out is too vague a statement. I can't stand it. I'd go as far as to say I loathe it, and I cringe every time I hear it said. It's a hopeful statement people throw around, without ever really defining it. What is being asked of people? What are they supposed to do or say? It's not clear, at all.

It's just too vague. It's similar to when someone says, 'Tell someone how you're feeling.' Great, yes, you should. It seems like a simple request, but how do you actually do it? This comes with its own form of stigma. Knowing what we know about psychosis apparently means we should be talking, we should be sharing. When we don't, we're at fault. You'll hear after or even during a crisis from people:

'Why didn't you tell me?'

This is a loaded question and isn't asked to show someone cares, but often as an insinuation you didn't fulfil your role, didn't do your 'job'. You didn't – you guessed it – 'reach out' as you've been told. We're expected to know how to do this, as if there's some guidebook handed to you. When we don't, we're often scolded and reprimanded for staying quiet.

It goes without saying that we all need to normalize asking for help, but it doesn't end there. We need to explore and understand how to ask for what we need. I've put together a few key phrases which explain exactly what you need, why you need it, and what's going on for you in that moment.

'I'm having hallucinations. I'm not sure what I need but I need someone to talk to.'

This explains simply how you're feeling and what's happening. Most importantly, it doesn't put pressure on you or the person you're contacting. You're explaining they don't need to fix anything or solve a problem; you just need someone to chat to. I like this one because often I can't pinpoint what I need to feel better, but I do know human connection will help.

'I'm struggling. Can we chat on the phone/facetime/etc. and come up with a plan together?'

This is a good one for the people close to us, because it gives them a sense of purpose. Just saying the words 'I'm struggling' can be massive. Leaving it hanging there in the middle of a conversation can feel oppressive and might be too much to manage. But following it up with a plan feels positive and shows you're in a place where you can be part of the process, even if you're unwell.

'Can you help distract me. Let's talk about anything.'

This is often what I need when I'm in a crisis or hearing voices. It's a simple statement which explains your state of mind, without having to go into detail. Distraction helps you focus on the conversation, rather than what you're experiencing. It doesn't matter what it's about – often it's just enough to hear another voice, or watching someone as they speak helps.

'I'm having a difficult time taking care of myself. Can you help with a few things?'

When we're having a difficult time, everyday tasks seem insurmountable. They build up and then we realize we can't cope. Asking for help, however small the ask, makes a massive difference. It might just be picking up some essentials from the shops, giving you a lift to a doctor's appointment, or something more, like helping you sort your finances.

'I'm really not feeling very good, and I'm worried about staying safe. Can you stay on the phone with me/stay with me/come over until I feel better?'

This is for when you're feeling distressed, having intrusive thoughts, or feeling suicidal. It's a way of telling someone you're feeling this way, without actually saying psychosis or the 's' word, which might freak some people out. Telling someone you trust them and want them to keep you company until the feeling passes will make them feel you value them, and it explains how serious the situation is.

Common warning signs of a psychotic episode

This isn't an exhaustive list, but some of the common signs many people with psychosis experience. It's a good idea to keep a diary of your moods, feelings, and what you did that day where a pattern of behaviour or moods might emerge, which can help you identify future warning signs.

- **Irritability.** Situations and people may become frustrating and irritating, and you feel everything touches a nerve.
- **Struggling to take care of yourself.** This could manifest in different ways. You might find it harder to prepare a meal or eat. Showering, brushing your teeth, and taking care of your appearance might become tough. Taking care of your home – like washing dishes, cleaning, and keeping it tidy – might start to become a massive effort.
- **Sticking to a routine gets harder.** Your regular daily routine might start to fall apart, and you struggle to get back on track.
- **Withdrawing.** You might find yourself withdrawing from friends, family, or social situations in general, preferring to stay home alone. If you live with family, roommates, or a partner, you may feel you need more time alone than usual.
- **Struggling to concentrate.** You might also find it hard to think clearly and have problems with focusing on tasks and concentration.
- **Feeling emotional or not at all.** Your emotions might

start to feel extremely intense and strange, or you may struggle to feel anything at all.

- **Work or education starts to suffer.** Due to the above, it may be difficult to focus on work or education.

Sara shared with me her warning signs, and how she acts on them.

I think it's understanding your own personal signs that things might be starting to go wrong. Or that things might be getting bad. A massive one for me is when I realize that I'm starting to withdraw from people I normally would be around a lot and things like that. And I think when you recognize those sorts of signs, and in yourself, you can then talk to the people around you and say, 'Look, I think I might be starting to get unwell, and I want to reach out for support and some help.' Or if there are specific things you think might help you, it's really difficult, because not everyone recognizes those things, and it's hard. But I'd say the best thing to do is before you get unwell is noticing things maybe – if you're withdrawing from people, if you're starting to not really look after yourself as much, or you're getting quite irritable or things like that. Even just small things – it's looking at that and being like, 'Right, what can I do to help myself before I get to the stage where I am really unwell?'

I think the main thing that's worked for me is reaching out to people. Not everyone's got people they can reach out to. It's a difficult one if you don't have much of a community. But I'd say even just anyone that you have in your life, or someone that is important to you, just to reach out to them and talk about how you feel or if you think things are starting to get bad.

I spoke to Sara about what it's like when you reach a point where you're too ill to reach out for support.

At that point, you're too far gone, and you just have to live it, don't you? You can't get yourself out of it when you're in it. When you're getting to that point, there are going to be things that you maybe notice are different about yourself, or at least I do, but I know that maybe I wouldn't have used to. And I maybe didn't notice that when I was really ill. But it totally depends on your own awareness of yourself. Or even if someone else notices something. So, like, maybe someone you work with, or someone you're friends with just says like, 'Oh, I noticed that you're not yourself', or there's something that's off, then maybe then that can be a thing for you to look at and be like, 'Right, maybe I need to do something to try and keep myself safe and well.'

Understanding your triggers

STRESS

This is a huge issue for people with psychosis, and probably the most common trigger for a psychotic episode. Stress can come from any part of your life, and why it's such a difficult trigger is that it can come out of nowhere. Whereas other triggers are easier to see coming, or to manage, stress can pop up when we least expect it. Focusing on the aspects of your life where stress is a factor can help you identify and learn to manage it. Keeping stress to a minimum, where you can, will mean you're in better shape for when stress unexpectedly erupts.

Hazel talked to me about crisis prevention and how vital it is.

I think a lot of it is about preventing crisis. Because once you're in a crisis, and once you're in psychosis, there's not much you can do, really. But there are things that you can do to prevent getting to that. A lot of it is figuring out what triggers it. For me, a lot of it seems to be stress. The more stress-lowering things I do, the longer I seem to go between episodes. So, I know I said that running doesn't fix it, because it doesn't. But I find that being outside and running can make me feel better when I'm already OK. So basically, there's a lot of stuff I do to maintain my current level of mental health, which isn't fantastic. But still, you know, I'm not about to die. That's really a low bar to set, isn't it? But that's my bar.

Sam told me what works for her when it comes to staying well.

I try to just keep stress levels low as stress is a big trigger for me. I also try to get enough sleep. It's different for everyone, but my meds keep me well. Without them, I imagine I would have to be hospitalized.

LACK OF SLEEP

Sleep is another trigger which is very common. There is a well-known link between a lack of sleep and psychotic experiences – either triggering a first episode or exacerbating a pre-existing issue. Disturbed sleep and psychosis can entail:

- trouble falling asleep
- staying up all night
- waking up after only a couple of hours of sleep and not being able to fall back to sleep
- only being able to sleep for an hour or two
- not being able to sleep at your usual time or when you're extremely tired.

Insomnia is a major issue and is categorized as when you're unable to sleep for at least three nights across a week. Often stress and insomnia are linked, so it's important to try to figure out the root cause of your sleeplessness.

Kody spoke to me about what works for him: taking medication, routine, and sleep.

My big thing is making sure that I am really safe about medication. So constantly keeping up with medication, and then being able to be in comfortable settings enough that I can decompress and be able to deal with any stress, which is always going to lead to more symptoms. So, trying to offset some of that by making sure that I'm taking enough time for myself, keeping on medication. And then I found that also everyone wants to talk about how much, anytime you hear about mental illness, people are always like, 'Oh, just eat better, exercise more.' That's not going to fix it. But I found in my own personal experience, that can help me just navigate my day-to-day life a little more. It's not going to fix any of my issues, but it'll help me feel a little more healthy and be able to navigate my daily routine. I think sleep is super important. Obviously, if you can get the full eight hours, I found that that helps me. It can be tough because I think with meds if you go to sleep later than you're supposed to, I still try to always take my meds at the same time. So, there are nights where I won't get as much sleep as I need to. But obviously sleep, I think, is a no-brainer for anyone who's worried about maintaining their mental wellbeing – making sure you get at least the recommended amount.

Everyone has responsibilities, and life sometimes gets in the way. It's a case of working it out and problem-solving the best way you can.

MANAGING SLEEP

If my sleep is disrupted for more than three days in a row (say, I get 2–3 hours a night) I can become very ill, very quickly. I've realized over the years that not sleeping is a major trigger, and I have to keep an eye on it, and try my best to get a good night's sleep. I'm also the type of person that when I'm depressed, I feel absolutely knackered all the time. All I want to do is sleep, and even when I get a good eight hours, I still feel exhausted.

What have I learned to help me sleep? First, it's not easy and the tips below won't solve the issue every single time. Sometimes you need to isolate the root cause for why you can't sleep and try to resolve that issue.

- **Get some exercise.** Honestly, wearing yourself out can help knock you out for the night. Tiring out your body lifts your mood and helps you sleep. It's best to exercise in the late afternoon or early evening if you can. It doesn't have to always mean going for a run or doing aerobics at home. Have a dance party in the lounge or get intimate with your partner.
- **Avoid screen time.** Blue screen is bad for sleep. Stay away from TV, your phone, computer, and laptop at least an hour before you go to bed. Instead, start your bedtime routine, read a book, even make a plan for the following day.
- **Get up at the same time every day.** Avoid taking naps during the day and try not to oversleep. Go to bed when you're tired but try to have a similar bedtime throughout the week.
- **Sensory items.** I'm talking body creams and mist sprays for your pillow. My lavender pillow is my best buddy when I'm struggling to sleep. If you don't have one, a hot

water bottle works just as well. It's comforting to have something warm and cuddly next to you – especially if you're sleeping alone.

- **Routine.** What this means is having a solid evening routine you stick to. It helps your body and mind relate certain tasks and sensory experiences to preparing for sleep. Washing your face, brushing your teeth, moisturizing your body are a great start. Incorporate calming hobbies and interests into your routine, such as reading a book in bed or in a quiet corner of the room you sleep in.

- **Reflect and plan.** Keep a journal and write down what you've done that day. It can help you sort through your thoughts and focus on something that might be worrying you, instead of those worries popping up when you're already in bed, trying to sleep. Writing is cathartic and can help you understand your anxieties and work through them. Listing on paper what you have to do tomorrow can stop you fixating on those plans when you're lying in bed.

- **Keep your bed for sex and sleep only.** Try not to spend too much time in your bedroom or specifically in your bed during the day and in the evenings. Try to keep your bedroom a cool, quiet space where you can relax. Spending time in bed working, browsing social media, or watching something can be a tempting habit to slip into, but it's not going to help us at night when we're trying to sleep.

HANDLING STRESS

As I mentioned earlier in this chapter, managing stress is all about learning to recognize it when it happens. We all react to stressors in our own way, so our view on what situations are actually stressful is always going to be different. Recognizing when we feel stressed and understanding the symptoms are an important first step. When we're stressed, we might feel tiredness and fatigue, headaches and tense muscles in our back or neck, and anxious and irritable. There might also be changes to our appetite and sleep, or using alcohol or other drugs to cope. Again, the way we react to stress will look and feel different for everyone.

- **Problem-solving.** When something is on your mind, like an unresolved problem, it can lead to stress. You know you need to make a change or a decision, but you just keep putting it off. I like to face problems head-on and as soon as I identify them, so that there's no time for the stress and worry to build up. Talking it through with someone and working together to come up with a solution is also an effective tactic.

- **Setting realistic goals.** This includes making small changes, or breaking goals down into smaller steps. Try not to change more than one thing at a time to reach a goal, or it might become too overwhelming a task. Make sure your goals are specific and clear – what are you trying to change and why? What do you want your goal to look like when you reach it? When you set a goal, make sure you're in a healthy place to begin with, or you could be setting yourself up for failure. Finally, when you've reached your goal, reward yourself with something you've been looking forward to.

- **Relaxation techniques.** Learning techniques such as deep belly breathing and progressive muscle relaxation will help you relax. Focusing on your breathing, music, or meditation are all examples of relaxation techniques. There are also light activities which can help us relax such as walking, stretching, dancing, yoga, and general sports and exercise.

- **Maintaining a healthy lifestyle.** There's the obvious such as eating a balanced diet, a good's night sleep, and getting plenty of fresh air and exercise. But a healthy lifestyle also includes socializing and communicating with friends and family and participating in recreational activities, hobbies, and interests.

DISTRACTIONS

I use distractions often when I'm stressed, or in the early stages of a psychotic episode. I find activities that keep my hands busy will help ground me in reality.

Sara explained how she tries to find joy in the activities she uses as distractions.

I'd say for yourself, I think it's important, not just for people around you I think, for yourself, even if you're recognizing things in yourself, where you're starting to feel unwell, it's so hard, I know, but finding things that you get joy from and leaning into those things a lot more than you maybe usually would. I've always found when I've started noticing that I'm not myself, I'll try, and a big thing for me is I sew, and I make stuff. When I can start to feel things getting a bit much, I lean into that and it's a big distraction for me, and it gives my thoughts somewhere to go rather than just sitting with them. It's all well and good, reading or listening to something. But even if you're not good at sewing or knitting or crocheting or whatever, even if it's shit, it gives your brain something to focus on. That takes away from the sort of bad stuff that's going on as well.

Distractions can include:

- sewing, knitting, or crocheting

- painting, sketching, or sculpting
- writing or journalling
- playing video games
- reading
- listening to music or a podcast in headphones
- playing a musical instrument
- gardening
- talking to a loved one.

ROUTINE

A routine is important in staying well. It keeps you focused and grounded and gives your days structure. Routine also helps us sleep and lowers stress when we know we have a plan for each day. Creating a routine is especially vital if you're at home often or don't work.

Chris explained how routine can be comforting.

Surround yourself with good people and practise a living routine so you have structure. It really helps me to wake up and do my routine. It's a comforting pattern while feeling alone or scared. It's grounding.

I particularly struggle with routine. I was unemployed for two and a half years because of mental illness. My lack of any routine made me feel sluggish and lacklustre, and I had little motivation to complete tasks or to look after myself. Without a routine, I didn't have much to ground me in reality and I had a few significant psychotic episodes during that time.

Michelle stressed the importance of routine even if they're small actions throughout your day.

Maybe in the morning, you go for a walk or something like that, take your meds, have your coffee, eat your breakfast, which could be a whole thing. Maybe you watch a morning show, which could be a thing. Or then you go to the park, come back from the park. Another thing. Just turn everything into something, you know, stay at home, watch TV all day, go just do something. Even if maybe the whole time you're doing that thing, you don't really talk to anyone, you're still doing something and not just being completely isolated. I think isolation is not good, really for you. So as long as you're around someone, or you're around other people, or you're somewhere else, I think that would be beneficial.

When I realized just how important routine was in keeping me well, I tried my best to embrace it. I still struggle now with routine – and that's OK. Knowing I have a plan is enough sometimes, and I don't beat myself up about it if I can't follow my routine. Usually, if my routine goes out the window, it's a warning sign I'm not well.

Libby spoke about how a routine can involve just your basic needs, if that's all you can manage.

I think something that I find is really important it's just looking after your basic needs. I find if I'm not looking after myself, if I'm not eating well, if I'm not drinking fluids, things like maintaining hygiene, taking medication, getting dressed. All those things I find really beneficial to helping me want to feel together. I find that when I let those things slip, I don't want to do anything else. That's when I start to isolate myself, and I stop talking to friends. I want to spend all day in bed, I want to come off my medication, I don't enjoy anything anymore. But my advice is focus on your basic needs. Because those are your foundation. Basic daily routine. But some days, even if all you can do is eat lunch, that is so much better than not doing any of it. And it's like I say, for me, getting fresh air really helps. But sometimes I can't even face stepping outside. So I just open a window. It's trying. And it's not just about getting your basic needs met. It's about doing it in whatever way works for you. Sometimes I can't brush my teeth. So I floss them. Because that's the only thing I can do. And that is still getting my needs met. It's just in a way that I can do it. It's what you can manage that day. It's better than just like going, 'Oh, I just can't do anything.'

Struggling with our basic needs can be difficult for people to understand. My partner finds it baffling how I can forget or not be bothered to brush my teeth. I try to explain sometimes I'm so unwell, the only things I'm able to do are the very basics.

Even if you can't face a routine that covers your entire day, then stick to a morning routine. It doesn't have to be complicated, but it sets us up to feel grounded, comforted, and calm for the day ahead. Here's an example of my morning routine when I was very unwell:

- Have a shower.
- Wash my face.
- Eat breakfast.
- Brush my teeth.
- Cuddle the cat!
- Read a book chapter/watch one episode of a favourite TV show/listen to an album.
- Go for a walk.

HOBBIES AND INTERESTS
As well as being a distraction from psychosis, hobbies and interests can help keep us well or provide comfort when we're unwell.

I asked Michelle, an artist with her own clothing brand, if she found art a therapeutic outlet which helps keep you well.

> Definitely. Because it just keeps me busy, gives me something to focus on. And I find it just fun and relaxing.

Chris shared how he uses art to work though his hallucinations.

> The things that I draw, I don't plan. And that's the weirdest part about it. And I've noticed it since I was a kid. I love to create things. And the way I've always done it since I was a little kid till now is very improvisational. I draw something and then I go, 'Oh, it'd be cool to put a flower here' – draws the flower. But then let's have someone sit over here on the side. And then let's have a tree. And so it happens very in the moment. All these pieces I do, I don't really plan them out. Because I find when I plan them out, then it's not as genuine to how I feel when I'm actually doing the piece. Because my art to me is it's spiritual. For me, it's a release, but it's also a reflection. I can see me in my own art – 'Oh, this is upsetting me' or 'Oh, this is something I should focus on.' It's like subconscious artwork.
>
> As we're talking right now, I'm just colouring in lines of a thing I was drawing earlier. It is therapy. It's pure therapy for me. It releases whatever angst or whatever I'm holding on to, and it helps me see things in a clearer way. And yeah, art has always been like a compass for me.

Hobbies and interests have helped me. Writing has always been a therapeutic outlet, but I find interests which are social are vital to keeping me well too. I love music, and going to gigs and watching live music encourages me to leave the house and see friends, all of which keeps me well.

Put together a crisis plan

Planning for a mental health crisis, or for your next psychotic episode, might feel like you're jinxing it, or you might think that assuming it will happen again is self-defeating. However, it does help you think about what could happen if you become ill and the support you'll need.

Creating a crisis plan helps you think about what you want to happen if you become very unwell and what support you need to have in place. Sometimes when we're extremely ill, we can't express our wants and needs, so having a plan lets the people around us know what help we need. Planning before things get rough means you'll have the right help and support ready to go, which gives you and your loved ones peace of mind.

Hazel shared a crisis plan they've put together and how it's helped.

I've made what's essentially my unofficial crisis plan, that two people have a copy of, and it has a list of red flags, it has a list of common delusions, common hallucinations, advice on things not to do, more than advice on things to do. So don't restrain me, don't lock me in the house, don't make me feel trapped in any way, or I will probably bite you. That's horrible to say to a friend, but it had to be in there! And there's also a bit at the bottom that I've signed that says that if you are concerned about me, even if I tell you not to, you have permission to contact and talk to the mental health services on my behalf. And I've signed that. Because I know in a crisis, I will be telling them not to. And I will shout at them a lot for doing it. And I'll be very angry at them. But I've signed it when I'm well. And sometimes if I'm really ill, there's nothing anyone who's not a professional is going to be able to do. In fact, there's very little a professional can do, but they can at least keep me alive. So yeah, that was a horrible conversation to have with someone. But needs must, I think. It's not been used yet, but it's reassuring that it's there. One of my massive fears is that while in an episode, I will do something, I will die. And I won't even know what's real when I die. I don't know why that makes dying worse. But I'm really scared of dying when I'm not in reality, probably accidentally because I'll be doing something stupid. So that was one of my biggest fears. So, it's alleviated that fear a little bit, at least as a backup plan.

Planning for challenging times is vital if you live with psychosis. Your crisis plan should be personalized, so it fits your needs. Here's a few things we can do to prepare for the 'just in case'.

BEFORE A CRISIS HITS

Talk to your doctor about treatment options and support in your area, and list what's available, along with important numbers and opening times for services. Make sure the contact details you have are up to date. Find out about local or online support groups and peer support services. People with similar experiences often have insights and can share advice and coping strategies.

Put together a box with items you find comforting and grounding and reminders of what works when you've struggled in the past. Fill it with items which distract your mind, such as your favourite book or movie and mementoes which remind you of happier times. You could also keep copies of contact information for services and support groups, or a list of people in your life who have helped in the past.

MAKE A PLAN WITH THE PEOPLE CLOSEST TO YOU

Put together an informal plan with your loved ones, so they

clearly understand what to do if you're in a crisis. It's essential they understand there's a chance you could have a crisis in the future, and even though it can be upsetting to think and talk about, having a plan in place means you'll get the help you need and want. Talk it through together, write down what you've decided, and ensure everyone has a copy.

The plan should include:

- contact details for your doctor and community support team if you're too unwell to contact them
- which treatments you'd prefer and which you do not want (e.g. being hospitalized)
- examples of what you find helpful when you're unwell.

A crisis plan is a guideline, not a legal document. Even if you've expressed a wish to not be hospitalized, if a medical professional believes it's needed you can still be sent to hospital involuntarily (sectioned).

You might want to choose someone you trust to advocate for you to doctors and other professionals, so your needs are met. They can express your views and wishes, and stand up for your rights. It can also be helpful to let your loved ones know what to look out for before a crisis hits. Explain what to watch out for, such as drastic changes to your mood and behaviour, and what these might look like for you.

Michelle spoke to me about how vital it is to have a good support team.

I would say have a good support team. Well, actually, having a good support team is really important. Including your doctor, your friends, your family – it's really important to have those people. And make sure you take your medicine. I would say those are the most important things. Make sure you have things to do during the day.

Jen explained the importance of medication and how it keeps her well.

I would say, take your meds! Take your meds on time, I would say. If you have any kind of feelings that are delusional or any kind of odd thoughts or feelings, speak to your mental health professional as soon as possible. Because the earlier you can deal with it, the quicker you can get treated for it. So don't hesitate to speak to your mental health team or professional as soon as possible. And just make sure you get enough sleep. Don't expose yourself to too much stress. All the usual caveats really. Eat healthily. If you can, do exercise.

Formalize your wishes with an advance statement

Sometimes when we're very ill, we're unable to make decisions about treatment. An advance statement is for these types of situations. It's a written statement explaining your wishes if you can't express them when you're having a mental health crisis. An advance statement is a way of formalizing your wishes that doctors and health care professionals will consider when deciding on treatment. It's not legally binding, but it should be looked at by the people in charge of your care.

It should include your treatment preferences, such as whether there are medications you don't want to take or if you wish to stay at home or in hospital. You might need to explain how a religious or spiritual belief should be part of your care. How you like to do things, such as if you prefer a bath or shower. Your likes and dislikes – a favourite scent, your favourite foods, or if you prefer being indoors or outdoors. Who you would like to deal with your bills and benefits, and who you'd like to look after any children or pets.

No one enjoys thinking about the worst-case scenario, and that's what a mental health crisis is. Planning for that 'what if' moment will make you feel more in control and calmer, knowing there's a plan in place.

Chapter 14

For People Who Want to Help

What not to say to someone with psychosis

Since being open about my experiences of psychosis, I've had many 'helpful' comments and sometimes some that are just downright insulting. So I've put together a list of the top comments that really shouldn't be said to anyone with psychosis.

Don't ask:

'Have you taken your meds?'

I find being asked this condescending and just rude. When I'm going through an episode of psychosis, being asked this question is not helpful. It actually makes me feel more paranoid than I already am.

Instead, you could ask:

'Is there anything I can do to help you remember to take your medication?'

Don't say:

'I had hallucinations when I took…'

OK, you may have taken a hallucinogen at some point, but it's an entirely different experience when you suffer with psychosis. You have no idea when the next episode may happen; you can't pick and choose how and when.

Instead, you could say:

'I had an experience a bit like this when I took… Is it similar? I'd like to understand what it's like for you.'

Don't ask:

'You must be really mental; shouldn't you be in hospital?'

I have lived with psychosis since I was a teenager and I've learned how to cope with the voices I hear. When I have delusions, I rely on my partner and family to keep an eye on me and my behaviour. It is possible to have an episode of psychosis and manage it without hospitalization. Believing I should be locked away is deeply stigmatizing and creates barriers to people discussing it. I might be having an experience that another person finds uncomfortable and doesn't fully understand, but that is on them to educate themselves, not for me to hide away.

Instead, you could ask:

'Do you have to be in hospital if you have a psychotic episode, or can you stay at home?'

Don't ask:

'It's just like having an imaginary friend, isn't it?'

I hear voices and no, it's not like having an imaginary friend. That's because children use their imaginations to create stories and scenarios. Psychosis feels like it's coming from an outside source, from outside your own inner monologue or imagination. Imaginary friends are often a source of comfort to the person. Although voices can sometimes be a positive experience, they can also be deeply frightening and disturbing.

Instead, you could ask:

'I don't know much about psychosis. Is it in any way like having an imaginary friend?'

Don't say:

'But I just want to fix it for you!'

Often the first thing someone will say to you is that they want to fix it; they want the problem to go away. Unfortunately, you can't fix another person. You alone can't fix psychosis. It's important to recognize that fact if you want to help someone with psychosis. When you do, you can move on from fixing and listen to what actually works for that individual. I've said to people that they need to get over the idea of 'fixing'. That they might have to learn to sit with not being able to find a solution and sit with being uncomfortable. Because it is uncomfortable. It might make you feel weird and awkward, but it's something you just have to deal with. Often, we think wanting to 'fix' a problem is proactive, but in this case it's counterproductive. What you can do is be there, listen, and communicate. Open communication about what does and doesn't help rather than taking matters into your own hands.

If you do or say the wrong thing, without first communicating what is or isn't OK, you may cause the person you're trying to help to isolate themselves from you and the support you could offer. Often when someone is extremely unwell, they aren't able to communicate effectively, so they withdraw instead.

Instead, you could say:

'I know it's not as simple as fixing it, but I want to help. Is there anything I can do?'

Don't say:

'That's such a stupid thing to believe!'

Confronting and arguing with someone about a delusion they are experiencing is not helpful. It may sound ridiculous to you, but to them, in a midst of a psychotic episode, it is very real. You can't convince someone to start looking at something in a different way. They're unwell and need understanding and support. Empathize with their situation and what they're going through. Try to focus on what might be troubling them and what you might be able to do to alleviate the stress they're feeling.

Instead, you could say:

'It must feel very real to you…but I'm struggling to understand.'

Don't say:

'Just stop thinking about it!'

This doesn't work. It might be frustrating trying to understand, but you can't just snap out of a psychotic episode. I literally can't stop thinking about the delusion or the voices I'm hearing. Often the person just needs to ride out the experience if they're having hallucinations. Focus on asking what you can do to help them. Be gentle in your questioning and stay calm.

Instead, you could say:

'It must be difficult to stop thinking about it. Let's do something together.'

How you can help before a psychotic episode happens

- Learn their warning signs.
- Understand their triggers.
- Help them keep a routine.
- Stay involved in their care.
- Put a crisis plan in place.

A crisis plan involves deciding on treatment options and hospital visits. You can also put together an informal plan with your loved one, where you set boundaries. By this, I mean what you can and can't deal with when they're in crisis. It's helpful to be honest and have a plan in place before a crisis hits. There is more about this in Chapter 13.

Kody explained how he has an informal plan in place in case of a crisis.

Me and my wife have planned for if symptoms get severe enough; we have backup plans for medication. I think that's part of being together. We've been together since before I experienced any symptoms. So we're going on six, seven, I don't even know, eight, maybe eight years now. We're going on a lot of years of navigating this illness together. So it's something where we've had a lot of the communication about what we need to do if I start to have symptoms. I'm quite a bit bigger than her too. So we've had the talk about if she were to feel unsafe, what should she do? Because she's five foot three, and I'm six foot one. And it's like we talked about earlier, people with mental illness aren't necessarily going to become violent. But if I were to get to the point of delusion, where she felt unsafe, we have plans for that.

It's vital to have that conversation if you're in a relationship. My partner and I, we've been together 13 years. We are very open to the point where we will say to each other, 'Just say it how it is!' We both know the score and what it means for me to have a psychotic episode. We have an informal plan in place, and he has numbers for my care team if I become very unwell. It's not perfect, and we're always learning better ways to deal with psychotic episodes, but it's effective in getting me the care and support I need.

I asked Jen if there's anything someone definitely shouldn't do or say to someone delusional.

So, when I was delusional, my dad used to confirm my delusions. I would say there's a tapeworm in my head. And he was like, 'Oh, my God, there is a tapeworm in your head.' And that would make me even more delusional. I would say don't indulge someone's delusions or symptoms, as hard as that is to do, because it's easy to just, if someone's really desperate, it's easy to indulge and confirm that delusion. But I'd say that's not helpful because they then become more delusional. It becomes like a shared delusion. There's a psychiatric word for that. There's a shared delusion between two people, or it could be more, but my dad and I definitely shared delusions. I guess my dad was quite elderly, quite vulnerable. So he was more likely to confirm my delusions.

How you can help during a crisis

BE GENTLE, KEEP CALM, AND DON'T PANIC

If someone is delusional or hallucinating, it's easy to get frustrated when what they're experiencing makes no logical sense to you. When they're telling you something that is obviously wrong or seeing or hearing things that aren't there, and you can see that they're obviously upset and distressed, you might feel as though you just want to shake it out of them somehow. You can't call them out and confront them, but you might feel as if you should. Don't do this. What your loved one is experiencing, in that moment, is very real to them. It's as real as you are, so trying to convince them otherwise will never work. What it will do is cause them more frustration and distress. Instead, stay calm. Speak to them gently and treat them how you would want to be treated if you felt distressed, paranoid, or confused and disorientated. It may take a great deal of patience and level-headedness if they keep repeating the same wild thoughts or ideas, so it's vital to take breaks when you need to. If you've read this book, you know there's no need to panic, and what they need is someone with a clear head and steady shoulders to guide them through.

Sara explained how simply being there for them can be just what's needed.

> I probably say the main thing is try not to give advice, because often it's not what people need to hear. And often, if you're trying to tell someone what to do to feel better, it doesn't help at all. I think it can often make people deflated, and they're being told what to do. I think the best thing you can do for someone

who's going through something like that is just being there for them. So even if you just go around and sit with them and watch something, even if it's going out somewhere for a bit, or I think just being there, because there's not much you can do… you can't just make someone stop having psychosis. That's not how it works. Sometimes it can be something you deal with for a long time. Sometimes it can be shorter than that. But as long as you are there for somebody in whatever capacity that is, and you're not trying to put your thoughts on someone because it doesn't help. I've had people say to me, like, 'Oh, you just need to do this.' And I'm like, 'Well, you don't actually understand because you're not in my head; you can't just make something stop.' I think the main thing is to be there, and do whatever that person might need that you're able to do. Just try to do those things. I think a good thing is always communication. And asking someone what they need, or what they feel they need. Or even if they don't know what they need, you can just say, 'Well, why don't I just come round? And we can just sit, or we can go for a walk or anything like that.' I've always found that really helpful.

Michelle echoes this sentiment but also stresses how crucial patience is when helping someone with psychosis.

Definitely be patient, be very patient, and just be there for them. If your loved one broke their leg, you would have to really help them. You would have to be patient with them. You wouldn't get frustrated with them because you can't do things. You know, you would help them out a lot because their leg's broken. Just treat them the same way as if they have something broken. Just because it's not physical, it doesn't mean it's not as debilitating.

Chris also explained the importance of patience.

> Be firm in your boundaries but don't get mad – that makes it
> worse. When dealing with psychosis, it's important to be patient,
> calming, and sincere. At least for me, that's what helps.

FOCUS ON THEIR FEELINGS

Talk about how they're feeling rather than the experience they're
going through. If they're agitated and frustrated, it might mean
they don't feel listened to or supported. If they're feeling stressed
or anxious, this might be why they're having an episode of psychosis. If they're extremely upset and distressed, it means they
need professional help as soon as possible. Focusing on their
feelings will help you decide what support they need and who
you should contact for further support and help. By making
them feel safe and secure, you can help guide them through
the experience. Remember, if you're concerned, find professional
support straight away.

Libby explains how helping to focus on the here and now
can be helpful.

> It's really difficult because a lot of people really want to work
> hard at dismantling the reality you've created. And while you
> shouldn't play into it either, it can also make you almost delve
> deeper into that reality, the more people push against it. I think
> something that has really helped me is instead of focusing on
> what I'm experiencing, focusing on actually helping me real-
> ize what is real. So focusing almost on grounding techniques,
> focusing on things that are actually real right now. To try to
> help me kind of dismantle the reality in my head. I think that's
> something that has been really helpful for me.

Sam believes compassion is the most important thing to have for someone who is psychotic.

> I'm very erratic during psychosis which makes it hard to say how someone could act to make things easier for me. I think just be compassionate. It's a very difficult time. I just want to feel understood like anyone else.

LISTEN

Try to understand and stay calm. When I say understand, I don't mean agreeing with their delusion or hallucination. Feeding into a delusion is not helpful and can exacerbate the problem. As I said, focus on their feelings and listen to what they're saying. Ask them what you can do to help. If they want you to do something that is part of the hallucination or delusion, tell them calmly you're not able to, and suggest practical help you can offer instead.

Kody told me how vital communication is in supporting someone with psychosis.

> I would say that it all has to start with communication, because everyone who experiences psychosis, schizophrenia, anything like that, we all experience it a little bit differently, which means we all have different needs for how to deal with it as well. So the best thing you can do is communicate with the loved one and be able to better understand what they need in those moments when they're struggling with psychosis or schizophrenia. If it's someone who is nonverbal or someone who is in the early stages of it, I always recommend just being there for that person until they are ready to get the help they need. Because forcing someone to get the help they need very rarely works, and usually leads to someone getting temporary help and ending up back

in the same position they were in. So just be there for them until they're ready to get the help they need is usually what I recommend.

Jen explained how listening to someone with psychosis is vital.

Just be really patient and listen to them and make sure you direct them to the nearest mental health professional. Because no matter how much you want to help them, you can't really. They need to see a mental health professional. So direct them to those services if you can. And just make sure they're being looked after, and make sure they're eating enough and drinking enough. And just look after them as best as you can really.

SHOW THEM RESPECT

Try not to be critical of their experience and what they're currently going through, and avoid being overprotective. You might feel that you know better and telling them what to do will help. However, it often creates a divide. You can respect their wishes to an extent. For instance, if they want to be supported in the home, rather than in hospital, you should respect that, unless they become a danger to themselves or others.

Hazel feels listening without judgement helps them when they are psychotic.

So that's hard, because every person will be different. Every person will have different things that will help them. So, I suppose the advice would be talk to the person and talk to them with an open mind and try not to make any assumptions or judgements. But just have an open honest conversation with the person.

Libby suggested helping her enjoy activities that are real.

Don't focus on telling me that something's not real over and over and over again, because that's not going to help me. And I feel like that won't help a lot of people. It just makes me really upset. Because I think it makes me feel like people think I'm crazy. And in that moment. I'm like, 'I know I'm not crazy. I know that what I'm experiencing is real.' Because for me it is real. So that doesn't help me, and I feel like it probably doesn't help a lot of people. But helping me to enjoy things that are real is something that has helped me come out of the other end of things.

This isn't an exhaustive list, only what I would find helpful and how I'd like to be treated when experiencing psychosis. Ultimately, everyone who goes through psychosis has a different experience of it, and their needs will not look the same as mine. Therefore, it's vital you talk to that person to get an understanding of their unique experiences before they become ill.

Look after yourself

Finally, it's important to acknowledge that it's tough to help someone going through psychosis. Sometimes there is nothing you can do but keep them safe until you can contact services that will offer the help they need. It can be challenging, upsetting, and sometimes distressing looking after someone going through psychosis. It's important to take care of your own wellbeing and health during these times.

What moment of support or friendship helped you?

I asked each interviewee if they could share a moment of support or friendship that helped them when they were unwell.

LIBBY

I was in university, and I was 19. I didn't really know what was real and what wasn't; I wasn't completely in an episode, but I wasn't not in one either. It wasn't new to me. I had an episode previously. And I had also heard voices before. But it wasn't something that was frequent or consistent. I still wasn't really sure I didn't know what was real. I didn't know what wasn't real. And everything was really confusing. And a friend, she sat down and just asked me what was going on, and wrote a list of everything that wasn't real, because she was able to know if something was real. For example, I thought there was a camera in my showerhead, and she was like, 'There definitely isn't.' She was able to write down, 'Libby thinks this, and it's not real.' So she did that for me. And then she made me a doctor's appointment. And she walked me there. It was on campus. It was literally a minute's walk, but she walked me there to make sure I went to it. And that was probably one of the biggest things that has helped me in terms of that. And then because of everything that came after it. All the support I got and the medication. I went to group CBT for psychosis after that, went on medication. Everything came from that, and I don't think I would have reached out for help if it wasn't for her.

CHRIS

My family had united together to help me from a terrifying delusion. All I needed was an ear to listen and a hug. I used to get mad at them asking me if I took my meds, but these days, I can see the love. So yes, authentic unconditional love. Being around unconditional love is a huge life saver for me.

HAZEL

My most recent one, people literally took my bank card off me. Because I thought I'd killed someone. And I was obsessed with finding out who I'd killed. I wanted to turn myself in to the police. But my plan had been to find out who I had killed, turn myself in to the police, tell them everything, and then go kill myself. Because I was a horrible person, because I killed someone. That was my plan. And I didn't even tell any of the people who are normally on my crisis plan this; I literally told someone on Twitter/X through DMs who then managed to – I'm a bit freaked out that they managed to do this – they managed to find my partner through Facebook and contacted him.

So they contacted him, and he didn't know what the hell to do. So he contacted a friend. And she recommended to not, well, you can't lock me up, because I will react badly to that. But to hide any access to money I have. Because we live in the middle of nowhere, the only way I'd be able to go do what I'd planned was to get a taxi. So if he hid all my access to money, I couldn't do that. I didn't have any money. So I couldn't go anywhere. And eventually, the thoughts passed – only lasted maybe two weeks. I don't know if that was the best way of handling it. But it worked. I'm still here. And the person he rang is the person whose family member has schizophrenia, so she's pretty good at this sort of stuff. She is a midwife herself. So she's always busy and she couldn't physically come around. But she could give him, you know, tips and advice, and she rang me constantly. Essentially, what happened is I just got distracted for two weeks.

JEN

I think my dad, he supported me emotionally, financially, in every way possible, really. He took me to appointments. He visited me when I was in prison. He visited me when I was in hospital. And he was just a constant source of…even though friendships end, I felt like my dad was an unconditional love. It didn't matter what I said or what I did. He was always there to support me. I was very lucky really to have him.

So, I was very lucky to have him and also my friend Emma. Even though I rang her up with delusions, she wouldn't panic. She wouldn't judge me. She was just really patient and listened to me and validated how I felt. And again, unconditional friendship.

SAM

Recently, I texted my friend about my delusions at 4 a.m. and the text must have woken him up because he replied. When I apologized for texting, he said he loved me just as I am. He's a cutie.

KODY

It's always been experiences with my wife. She has been very good at figuring out that the best way to help me in those moments is actually not to draw attention to my hallucinations or even to reassure me that they're not there. I really prefer distractions. And one example specifically was early on in our relationship before I even realized that that's what I needed. She identified I was having hallucinations, and instead of reassuring me they weren't there, she distracted me by talking about something completely unrelated to what was going on. And then after she got my attention away long enough, she suggested I go play a video game. Video games, I have found, have always been really good for me, because they're both auditory and visual stimulants. So it's a very good distraction. And so she was able to get me away from what I was experiencing just by offering a distraction unrelated to what was going on. And that's when we identified that that would work best for me.

MICHELLE

My college lacrosse coach was really supportive. Having her support me in college was very helpful. It was before I was on the medication I'm on now, before I was diagnosed with schizophrenia. She kept me on track, made sure that I took my meds and was just helpful if there was an issue.

SARA

I'd say the last time I was really unwell was probably a couple of months ago. And I remember I was in crisis. And I just felt like everything was enough. And I remember my friend Tim – he owns a vintage shop. And that's something I'm into. And he said, why don't you just come down and you can just sit, and I can show you nice things. And he didn't ask questions. He wasn't intrusive. And he literally just sat with me and made me realize that just existing doesn't have to be horrible. And there are so many nice things. And I love when people don't try to ask you about every single thought you're having. Because that can be triggering in itself. I think it's when they recognize, you're in that state, and they know the things that you like, that will make you feel even just a little bit better. I think that for me was what I needed at that moment.

For me, it has to be a moment from my partner, Jimi. He loves his sleep and is an absolute grump in the morning if he doesn't get a good night's rest. There was a period where I was extremely depressed and struggling to sleep, with insomnia kicking my arse. One of those nights, I was lying wide awake in bed, when I heard a voice, as clear as if Jimi had woken up, turned over in bed, and spoken to me. But it didn't sound anything like him. The voice sneered at me, loudly and full of malice, which sent a shiver down my spine:

'I can see you.'

I sat bolt upright in bed. I felt paralyzed with fear as I scanned the room for any movement and the source of the noise. When I could, I poked Jimi awake. Ignoring the grumbles, I explained what had happened. It was Jimi's turn to sit up in bed, and he snapped into action, no further explanation needed. We both got out of bed and sat in the lounge together. Jimi knew I needed distraction, so he started talking; I couldn't tell you now what about, but it was enough. It kept my mind off the voice I'd heard, and I could focus on the sound of Jimi's voice, even if I was too overwhelmed to take part in a conversation. That night was maybe six years ago, but it's etched in my mind, a cherished memory of someone doing their best for me.

Many of these moments might not mean much to the person actioning them, but trust me, they mean the world to the person going through it. It's a cliché, but small actions really do make a difference, because our view of what's a 'big' or 'small' gesture changes from person to person. You can never be 'too much' or do too much for someone with psychosis.

The Interviewees

Many of the interviewees use social media, podcasts, and You-Tube to raise awareness of psychosis. Follow them to find out more!

Sara Davidson is a charity shop manager and also has a small vintage business making clothing and accessories out of 1960s and 1970s textiles. Sara makes most of her own clothes and learning to sew has played a major part in helping them live with chronic mental illness. Sara is also a passionate disability activist and psychiatric abolitionist, and is active within the trade union movement. She cares a lot about people and animals, and has a particularly cute cat who is pictured a lot on her Instagram @ssaradavidson, which also includes her life of colour!

Christopher Grant is a Mi'gmaw filmmaker from Pabineau First Nation, New Brunswick. Inspired by the intense absurdity of life and death, Chris animates to express the humour and terror of existence. He has worked with the NFB's Hothouse project, and his work has been exhibited at galleries, museums, and film festivals internationally. He is also known for his role on TikTok as Xorad (@xoradmagical), where he creates art and answers questions all relating to his experiences with schizophrenia and daily life. Instagram @xoradmagical

Kody Green (he/him) is a 28-year-old with a diagnosis of undifferentiated schizophrenia. Kody is also the founder of a non-profit, a motivational speaker, and content creator with more than one million followers across social media platforms. He has struggled in the past with drug addiction, incarceration, and serious mental health issues.

In order to be a better advocate and speaker, Kody has been trained as a peer support specialist, recovery coach, and suicide prevention specialist. Kody shares his stories about his struggles and how to navigate through recovery, mental health issues, and life after incarceration. He chooses to pursue motivational speaking and mental health advocacy for schizophrenia awareness, drug recovery, and second-chance opportunities because he has dealt with these struggles in his own life. Instagram: @schizophrenichippie; TikTok: @schizophrenichippie; YouTube: @SchizophrenicHippie; Facebook: @KodyGreen.

Michelle Hammer is a schizophrenia activist and spends her time passionately fighting stigma. She is an NYC native featured in the WebMD documentary *Voices*, which was nominated for a Tribeca X Award at the Tribeca Film Festival. Michelle was diagnosed with schizophrenia at 22, after a misdiagnosis of bipolar at age 18. At 27, Michelle decided to use her fearless personality to do something that could benefit the mental health community. In May 2015, she founded a mental health-focused clothing brand. Schizophrenic.NYC is a clothing brand with the mission of reducing stigma by starting conversations about mental health. Website: www.Schizophrenic.NYC; Instagram: @schizophrenic.nyc; TikTok: @schizophrenic.nyc; Youtube: @schizophrenicnyc; Facebook: @schizophrenicnyc; Twitter/X: @Schizophrenicny.

Hazel Cornhill is a mental illness campaigner and podcaster with a degree in Neuroscience, who happens to also have schizoaffective disorder. When not campaigning, they can usually be found out running or hiking on local trails, or studying towards their second degree in Psychology. On social media, they can be found on Twitter/X (@AnLasair) and on Instagram (@an.lasair).

Libby-Mae Ford is a disabled third-year psychology student living in South Wales with her fiancée, Molly. She works in the NHS using her lived experience to help to improve services, and she hopes to train as a clinical psychologist after her master's. She loves to read, paint, and write, and when she's not doing any of these, you can find her cuddling cats and watching *Grey's Anatomy*. Libby has struggled with various mental illnesses over the course of her life and uses her social media to spread awareness and help others feel less alone. You can find Libby @hello.itslibby on Instagram and @libby4000 on Twitter/X.

Jen McPherson is a freelance journalist and writer. She is currently studying for a diploma in Multimedia Journalism at News Associates in Manchester. She has written articles for the *Guardian* and *Telegraph* newspapers. She has written a chapter about her experience with bipolar disorder in a book due to be published by HarperCollins in May 2023. She won the Jessica Kingsley Writing Prize in 2023. She tweets at @tokyoslumbers.

Sam has a degree in English literature and likes video games, contemporary illustration, and rainbow dungarees!

Resources

USA

National Alliance on Mental Illness (NAMI)
www.nami.org/home
NAMI Helpline at 800-950-6264

Black Emotional and Mental Health Collective (BEAM)
https://beam.community

Call BlackLine
www.callblackline.com
Helpline at 1-800-604-5841

Students with Psychosis
https://sws.ngo

The Trevor Project
www.thetrevorproject.org

Helpline at 1-866-488-7386
Text Us: 678-678

Mental Health America (MHA)
https://mhanational.org
Call or text 988 or chat 988lifeline.org

UK

Rethink Mental Illness
www.rethink.org

Samaritans
www.samaritans.org
Helpline at 116 123

Mind
www.mind.org.uk
Mind Infoline: 0300 123 3393

Black Minds Matter UK
www.blackmindsmatteruk.com

Young Minds
www.youngminds.org.uk
text SHOUT to 85258

Action on Postpartum Psychosis (APP)
www.app-network.org

Positive media representations of psychosis

DOCUMENTARIES
David Harewood: Psychosis and Me, BBC
My Mind and Me, Apple TV

PODCASTS
A History of Delusions, BBC Radio 4
All in the Mind, BBC Radio 4
Coffee and Psychosis
Inside Schizophrenia
Mind Podcast
Reality Tourists

About the Author

Kai Conibear was diagnosed with bipolar disorder in 2012 and has been blogging about his experiences ever since. His blog has an international readership and he was shortlisted in the Digital Champion category at the Mind Media Awards in 2018. Kai is a freelance writer, focusing on mental health, and is based in Reading, UK. He can be found on Instagram and TikTok as @kconibearwriter, and on Twitter/X as KConibear.

References

American Psychological Association (2014) Incarceration nation. *Monitor on Psychology 45*, 9. www.apa.org/monitor/2014/10/incarceration

Bürgy, M. (2008) The concept of psychosis: Historical and phenomenological aspects. *Schizophrenia Bulletin 34*, 6, 1200–1210. https://doi.org/10.1093/schbul/sbm136

Drake, R.J., Addington, J., Viswanathan, A.C., Lewis, S.W. *et al.* (2016) How age and gender predict illness course in a first-episode nonaffective psychosis cohort. *Journal of Clinical Psychology 77*, 3, e283–e289. https://doi.org/10.4088/jcp.14m09369

Healy, C., Brannigan, R., Dooley, N., Coughlan, H. *et al.* (2019) Childhood and adolescent psychotic experiences and risk of mental disorder: A systematic review and meta-analysis. *Psychological Medicine 49*, 10, 1589–1599. https://doi.org/10.1017/S0033291719000485

HM Inspectorate of Probation (2021) A joint thematic inspection of the criminal justice journey for individuals with mental health needs and disorders. www.justiceinspectorates.gov.uk/cjji/wp-content/uploads/sites/2/2021/11/Mental-health-joint-thematic-report.pdf

Isham, L., Griffith, L., Boyland, A.-M., Hicks, A. *et al.* (2019) Understanding, treating, and renaming grandiose delusions: A qualitative study. *Psychology and Psychotherapy 94*, 1, 119–140. https://doi.org/10.1111/papt.12260

Khalifeh, H., Oram, S., Osborn, D., Howard, L.M. and Johnson, S. (2016) Recent physical and sexual violence against adults with severe mental illness: A systematic review and meta-analysis. *International Review of Psychiatry 28*, 5, 433–451. https://doi.org/10.1080%2F09540261.2016.1223608

McManus, S., Bebbington, P., Jenkins, R. and Brugha T. (eds) (2016) *Mental health and wellbeing in England: Adult Psychiatric Morbidity Survey 2014.* Leeds: NHS Digital. https://files.digital.nhs.uk/pdf/q/3/mental_health_and_wellbeing_in_england_full_report.pdf

Mind (2018) GP mental health training survey: Summary. www.mind.org.uk/media-a/4414/gp-mh-2018-survey-summary.pdf

Mueser, K.T., DeTore, N.R., Kredlow, M.A., Bourgeois, M.L., Penn, D.L. and Hintz, K. (2020) Clinical and demographic correlates of stigma in first-episode psychosis: The impact of duration of untreated psychosis. *Acta Psychiatrica Scandinavica 141*, 2, 157–166. https://doi.org/10.1111/acps.13102

NAMI (2023) Psychosis. www.nami.org/About-Mental-Illness/Mental-Health-Conditions/Psychosis

National Collaborating Centre for Mental Health (2021) Psychosis and Schizophrenia in Children and Young People: Recognition and Management, National Clinical Guideline No. 155, commissioned by The National Institute for Health and Care Excellence. Published by The British Psychological Society and The Royal College of Psychiatrists. www.nice.org.uk/guidance/cg155/evidence/full-guideline-pdf-6785647416

National Institute of Mental Health (2023) Understanding Psychosis. www.nimh.nih.gov/sites/default/files/documents/health/publications/understanding-psychosis/23-MH-8110-Understanding-Psychosis.pdf

National Institute on Drug Abuse (2020) Criminal Justice DrugFacts. https://nida.nih.gov/publications/drugfacts/criminal-justice

Rethink Mental Illness (2023) Young people and psychosis: Our new research says they are unaware of warning signs despite being most at risk. www.rethink.org/news-and-stories/media-centre/2018/sep/young-people-and-psychosis-our-new-research-says-they-are-unaware-of-warning-signs-despite-being-most-at-risk

Reynolds, E.H. and James V. Kinnier Wilson (2014) Neurology and psychiatry in Babylon. *Brain 137*, 9, 2611–2619. https://doi.org/10.1093/brain/awu192

Royal College of Psychiatrists (2021) National Clinical Audit of Psychosis.

www.rcpsych.ac.uk/docs/default-source/improving-care/ccqi/national-clinical-audits/ncap-library/employment-physical-health-spotlight-2021/ncap-spotlight-audit-report-on-employment-2021-(2).pdf?sfvrsn=71deb31f_4

Smith, R.C. (2020) We must train physicians who provide mental health care. *Psychology Today*, 19 December. www.psychologytoday.com/us/blog/patient-zero/202012/we-must-train-the-physicians-who-provide-mental-health-care

Time to Change (2015) Attitudes to Mental Illness: 2014 Research Report. www.mind.org.uk/media-a/2141/attitudes-to-mental-illness-2014-report-annexes-1.pdf

de Vries, B., van Busschbach, J.T., van der Stouwe, E.C.D., Aleman, A. *et al.* (2019) prevalence rate and risk factors of victimization in adult patients with a psychotic disorder: A systematic review and meta-analysis. *Schizophrenia Bulletin 45*, 1, 114–126. https://doi.org/10.1093/schbul/sby020